HOMECOOKED FEASTS

FAVOURITE CELEBRATORY RECIPES FROM AUSTRALIAN KITCHENS

RECIPES SELECTED BY MAGGIE BEER
AND VALLI LITTLE
FOREWORD BY IAN 'MACCA' MCNAMARA

ABC
Books

ABC Books has made every attempt to contact all contributors to this book. Please contact ABC Books at the address below if it is apparent we have only your email address.

Published by ABC Books for the
AUSTRALIAN BROADCASTING CORPORATION
GPO Box 9994 Sydney NSW 2001

First published in November 2008

ISBN 978 0 7333 2272 3.

Cover and internal design by Christabella Designs
Typeset in 10 on 13.5pt Sabon by Kirby Jones
Printed and bound in Australia by Ligare, Sydney

2 4 5 3 1

CONTENTS

FOREWORD

To me, homecooked means good food and good company, and there's no better company than the people you love. The most memorable meals I've ever eaten have been homecooked, courtesy of my mother. She took some great produce and cooked it with love, and it gave her food a special flavour.

When there's a special occasion, and family and friends gather round to celebrate something — a birthday, a wedding, a homecoming, or Christmas — then it's great to have a good excuse to have a big feast.

What's special about this book is that it has lots of celebratory recipes that have come from ABC Local Radio listeners all over Australia. Mums, dads, sisters, brothers, grandmas and grandpas; they've all given up a recipe for their favourite things to cook and eat on special occasions. Many of these recipes have been handed down from generation to generation, and because of that, there are a lot of great stories surrounding them. Stories of partings, homecomings, births and marriages, and all those occasions that give us the chance to have a party with our families and friends and celebrate being with them and eating some great Aussie food!

Ian 'Macca' McNamara

INTRODUCTION

Just about every special occasion we know is celebrated in one way or another by sharing good food with family and friends, and these traditions are not bound by race or culture. Whether it is Christmas, a wedding, a birthday or even celebrating a good harvest, sharing food together becomes one of life's great pleasures and it is often the basis of some of our happiest memories.

Helping to select the recipes for this book was no easy task — not only because all of them sounded so delicious I couldn't wait to get into the kitchen and try them myself — but because so many of them came with such wonderful anecdotes and stories from Australian lives, and their provenance was often the reason for them being so well treasured. These are dishes whose poetry comes from their evocative names and stories, and they have given us a very special insight as to why each means so much to a particular family.

Whether the feast you are planning is a formal or casual affair, this book is a wonderful inspiration packed full of recipes that you will enjoy cooking and certainly everyone will enjoy eating.

Happy feasting!

Valli Little
Food Director
delicious. magazine

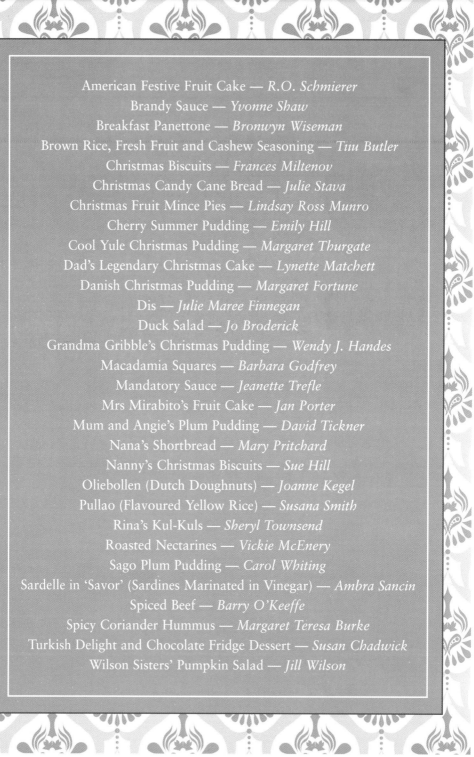

CHRISTMAS

AMERICAN FESTIVE FRUIT CAKE
Serves 10–15

This recipe appeared in a magazine when I was searching for a different Christmas cake about forty years ago. When I made and took it home to my family during the festive season it was a real hit. Each Christmas, family, friends and neighbours would say to me, 'Did you bring THAT CAKE again?'. It is rich and cut into reasonably small pieces goes a long way among 10–15 people.

INGREDIENTS

250 g dates, pitted
250 g glacé pineapple
125 g glacé apricots
125 g each of red and green glacé cherries
250 g brazil nuts
2 eggs
½ cup (100 g) brown sugar
1 tablespoon rum
1 teaspoon vanilla essence
90 g butter, softened
½ cup (75 g) plain flour
½ teaspoon baking powder
pinch of salt
12 tablespoons rum or brandy, extra

METHOD

Preheat the oven to 150°C. Grease and line a 23 x 12 cm loaf tin.

Chop the dates, pineapple and apricots into fairly large pieces, but leave the cherries and nuts whole. Mix well.

Beat the eggs until light and fluffy, add the sugar, rum, vanilla and soft butter. Continue beating until well blended.

Sift the flour with the baking powder and salt, add to the creamed mixture with the fruit and nuts, and mix well. Spoon into the prepared tin. Bake for approximately 1½ hours, or until the cake is firm to touch and a skewer comes out clean. The cake may have a surface layer of melted butter — on cooling this will settle and moisten the cake. Remove from the oven, and while still hot, pour extra rum or brandy over. Cool in the tin standing on a wire rack.

R.O. Schmierer, Singleton, NSW

BRANDY SAUCE
Serves 8

This recipe was given to me by a neighbour on my first Christmas spent in Tottenham, NSW, back in the 1960s. I have not had it anywhere else and I have been cooking this ever since. It is very popular and unfortunately not enough people know about it.

INGREDIENTS
125 g butter
2 cups (400 g) brown sugar
60 ml brandy
4 eggs, separated
1½ cups (375 ml) cream

METHOD
Cream the butter, stir in the sugar gradually and then add the brandy very slowly. Add the well beaten egg yolks and the cream. Cook in the top of a double saucepan until thick, stirring constantly. Remove from the heat and leave to cool.

Fold in the stiffly beaten egg whites just before serving. Beautiful with Christmas pudding.

Yvonne Shaw, by email

BREAKFAST PANETTONE

Serves 4 well-satisfied adults

This family tradition came about when looking for something slightly indulgent but simple to have for breakfast on what is almost always a warm to hot Adelaide Christmas day. The smell is almost as good as the taste and it is best combined with coffee and present opening.

INGREDIENTS

1 panettone (or 1 small one per person)
butter or marscapone
cherry or other dark jam (optional)
mixed fresh berries (optional)

METHOD

Cut the panettone into thick slices and lightly toast under the grill. Spread with butter or marscapone while still warm. Top with jam or mixed fresh berries.

Bronwyn Wiseman, Watson, ACT

Brown Rice, Fresh Fruit and Cashew Seasoning
Serves 8–10

This recipe was given to me, by phone, by my mother Linda who is now in a nursing home. Her recipe contained dried fruit such as apples, apricots and prunes, which were soaked overnight in cider or apple juice.

Ingredients

30 g unsalted butter
3 tablespoons olive oil
1 large white onion, finely chopped
2 garlic cloves, crushed
4 large ripe apricots, diced
4 ripe blood plums, diced
½ cup (125 ml) tart or homemade red plum jam
3 cups (555 g) steamed brown rice
½ bunch flat-leaf parsley, finely chopped
2 tablespoons finely chopped dill
sea salt and freshly ground black pepper
2 tablespoons finely chopped chives
¾ cup (115 g) toasted cashews

METHOD

Preheat the oven to 180°C.

Melt the butter with 2 tablespoons of the olive oil. Sauté the onion and garlic over low heat until transparent.

Add the apricots and plums to the onion mixture, cook for about 10 minutes.

Add the plum jam, brown rice, extra tablespoon of olive oil, parsley and dill. Season to taste with salt and pepper.

Place into a greased ovenproof serving dish and bake for 30 minutes. Decorate with chives and cashews if serving immediately.

If serving the dish the following day, reheat in a moderate oven for about 20 minutes, before serving. If reheating in a microwave oven, add the cashews after reheating.

Delicious with roast pork and poultry.

Tiiu Butler, Inverell, NSW

CHRISTMAS BISCUITS

24–30 biscuits

For us it just wouldn't be Christmas without these scrumptious little biscuits. The tradition started with me preparing these biscuits, which I placed in pretty little baskets or jars to give to friends as a Christmas gift. This is now ongoing and these biscuits are truly sought after by everyone.

INGREDIENTS

250 g butter
1 teaspoon vanilla extract
½ cup (60 g) icing sugar, sifted
¾ cup (75 g) walnuts or hazelnuts, finely chopped
2 cups (300 g) plain flour
icing sugar, extra

METHOD

Preheat the oven to 180°C and grease 2 baking trays.

Cream the butter, vanilla and icing sugar. Add the nuts and flour. Mix together into a dough then roll into small balls in palms of hands.

Place onto lightly greased baking trays.

Leave in little 'snowball' shapes or press down lightly to flatten. Bake for about 20 minutes.

Remove from the trays and allow to cool until the biscuits are barely warm, then roll in the extra icing sugar (if biscuits are too hot the icing sugar will melt). When quite cold roll in more extra icing sugar. Store in an airtight container. Alternatively, put in a Christmas decorative basket and give to your friends.

Frances Miltenov, Malvern, VIC

CHRISTMAS CANDY CANE BREAD

Makes 3 loaves

Every year on Christmas Eve day I make a batch of this candy cane bread. We enjoy one of the canes with coffee and drinks on Christmas Eve, the extra 2 are given as gifts to friends or helpful neighbours or kept in the freezer for family members who cannot join us this Christmas. Any leftover is consumed for brekkie on Christmas Day.

INGREDIENTS

2 cups (500 g) sour cream
30 g fresh yeast (or 2 tablespoons dry yeast)
½ cup (125 ml) warm water
60 g soft butter
⅓ cup (75 g) sugar
2 teaspoons salt
2 eggs, lightly beaten
6 cups (900 g) plain flour, approximately
1½ cups (270 g) diced dried apricots
1½ cups (300 g) maraschino cherries, cut in half
melted butter, to brush

Glaze
2 cups (300 g) icing sugar
2 tablespoons water
few drops of vanilla essence

2 packets mixed green and red glacé cherries, to decorate

Method

Heat the sour cream over low heat until lukewarm. Dissolve the yeast in the warm water in a large bowl. Stir in the sour cream, butter, sugar, salt, eggs and 2 cups of the flour. Beat until smooth.

Mix in enough flour to make the dough easy to handle (leave ½ cup for kneading).

Turn the dough on to a floured surface and knead until smooth. Place into greased bowl, turn greased side up, cover and leave to rise in a warm place for 1 hour.

Preheat the oven to 180°C.

Combine the apricots and maraschino cherries in a small bowl. Punch the dough down and divide into 3 equal balls. Roll each ball out on a floured surface to form a rectangle about 35 x 25 cm. Using kitchen scissors, make cuts in the dough along the 35 cm side. They should be at 2 cm intervals, about 6 cm into the dough leaving an uncut strip down the centre length.

Place one-third of the fruit mixture down the centre. Take the cut strips and plait over the centre in a crisscross fashion, tucking under the ends.

Carefully place onto a large baking tray, and turn the end into a hook to look like a candy cane. Repeat with the remaining dough.

Cover and set aside in a warm place for 30–40 minutes. Bake for 15–20 minutes or until golden.

While hot, brush with the melted butter. Transfer to wire racks to cool completely.

To make the glaze, mix the icing sugar, water and vanilla. Drizzle over the candy canes in a zigzag or circular fashion.

Cut the green glacé cherries into quarters. Before the glaze sets, place the red cherries in clusters of 3 along the canes, using the glaze as 'glue'. Place quarters of the green glacé cherries between the red cherries to look like holly leaves.

Julie Stava, Tocumwal, NSW

CHRISTMAS FRUIT MINCE PIES

(This quantity makes approx. 18 pies so I usually make double the
quantity and freeze them)

*When my mother was married in Brisbane in 1936, she did not
have any family to teach her the cooking skills she needed as a
new bride. The grandmother of one of her friends came to her
rescue and gave Mum some of her old family recipes and taught
Mum how to make them. This recipe has been a favourite in our
family for as long as I can remember.*

INGREDIENTS

Fruit Mince
125 g butter
1 cup (220 g) raw sugar
1 tablespoon mixed spice
500 g good quality mixed fruit (with real glacé cherries!)
50 g chopped almonds
½ cup (125 ml) rum
2 large green cooking apples, peeled and chopped

Sweet Pastry
125 g butter
1 teaspoon vanilla extract
½ cup caster sugar
1 egg
1½ cups (225 g) plain flour
½ cup (150 g) self-raising flour
½ cup (60 g) cornflour

egg white, lightly beaten

Method

To make the fruit mince, cream the butter thoroughly. Beat in the sugar and mixed spice. Add the other ingredients, except for the apple. Pack into a sterilised screw top jar for use as required. Make at least two or three weeks before you need it and keep in the fridge. Add the prepared apple just as you use the fruit mince.

Preheat the oven to 180°C and grease patty tins.

To make the sweet pastry, cream the butter and vanilla and gradually beat in the sugar. Beat in the egg.

Sift the flours several times. Add gradually to creamed mixture (The mixture will become stiff and you will have to estimate whether it will take all the flour. I usually find that about ½ cup flour is left, which I use to roll out the pastry). DO NOT ADD ANY LIQUID.

Roll the dough out thinly. Cut to the right size with a fluted biscuit cutter and fit carefully into the prepared tins. Fill with the fruit mince and brush the edges with the egg white. Press the top of each pie on carefully. Brush with the egg white and cut a vent in the top.

Bake for about 15 minutes or until the pastry is a pale golden colour. Serve with cream or ice cream. I freeze all the pies and defrost as required.

Lindsay Ross Munro, St Ives, NSW

CHERRY SUMMER PUDDING
Serves 8–10

Our home-grown cherries are ripe at Christmas and are always eaten for breakfast on the day. This dessert has become a Christmas lunch favourite.

INGREDIENTS
1 kg cherries, pitted
sugar, to taste
1 teaspoon almond essence
4 tablespoons kirsch or brandy
1 large panettone or brioche, sliced
double cream and grated dark chocolate, to serve

METHOD
Stew the cherries in the sugar and a few tablespoons of water until soft. Remove from the heat and add the almond essence and kirsch.

Line a large pudding basin with slices of panettone or brioche and drizzle with some of the cherry liquid. Fill the lined bowl with the cherries then finish with another layer of panettone or brioche. Refrigerate when cool and leave overnight before serving. Serve with the double cream rippled with chocolate.

Emily Hill, Mt Rowan, VIC

Cool Yule Christmas Pudding

Serves 8–10

This recipe has been made by me every year for the past thirty-one years. Each year from November onwards I have requests for it from my family. They tell me they are happy in the knowledge that each year Christmas will be secure, predictable and utterly delectable feast of Christmas fare. It is first most important to gather the correct utensils — this may be difficult, but ask around. In this case you will need a '70s green Tupperware container that was produced to hold an iceberg lettuce. It is the perfect shape and size for your purposes. In my house it has never been used for any other purpose except for the production of the Christmas pudding. After my mother died I gained her lettuce container too, and as a result, as my family grew, I can make two puddings each year. Unfortunately, the container that Tupperware currently makes for their lettuce is not suitable.

I will concede that a suitable alternative container is an ordinary pudding bowl, but try to use an heirloom one as the final result will reflect this love!

INGREDIENTS

- 250 g cherries
- 250 g raisins
- 200 ml Bundaberg rum
- 250 g packet chocolate-covered scotch finger biscuits
- 2 tablespoons very good quality cocoa powder
- 50 g unsalted butter, melted
- 2 litres very best vanilla ice cream (traditionally I use Streets Blue Ribbon, as I always have)

Method

Cut the cherries in half and discard the pips. Soak the cherries and raisins in the rum for at least two days — the cherries will change colour, don't worry about this.

When you are ready to make the pudding, blitz the biscuits very finely in a food processor, add the cocoa and melted butter, and carefully pat the mixture all around the inside of the pudding container you are using. Persevere, it will stick eventually! Place the container in the fridge while you do the rest.

Working quickly, combine the ice cream with the cherry mixture, and fold gently to evenly distribute the fruit. Take the prepared crust from the fridge and fill the pudding bowl with the ice-cream mixture. Strangely, it will fit — this always amazes me. Place the plastic lid on the container, if you are lucky enough to be using the green Tupperware lettuce keeper, or cover the top of the bowl with a double thickness of foil and put an elastic band around it. Refreeze.

On Christmas day, take from the freezer and dip the bowl into hot water for about 30 seconds, then invert onto a serving plate.

Decorate the top with holly and take to the table.

Stand back and receive the compliments!

Margaret Thurgate, Alstonville, NSW

DAD'S LEGENDARY CHRISTMAS CAKE

Makes 1 cake

My father made this cake every year when we were growing up as children. Now we are mothers with children of our own, Dad still makes a cake for each of us to share over the Christmas period. When we were little we used to mix the ingredients, now the grandchildren are invited over to mix the cakes.

INGREDIENTS

7 eggs
250 g (1¼ cups) brown sugar
1 tablespoon coffee essence
2 cups (300 g) plain flour
¼ cup (30 g) self-raising flour
1 teaspoon salt
2 teaspoons mixed spice
250 g copha
500 g mixed fruit
125 g chopped dried apricots
50 g glacé cherries, chopped
60 g blanched almonds
250 g pitted dates, chopped
6 tablespoons sweet sherry or brandy

METHOD

Preheat the oven to 150°C. Line a 20 cm square or round cake tin with baking paper 4 cm higher than the tin.

In a large bowl beat the eggs and gradually add the brown sugar and coffee essence, set aside.

the flours, salt and mixed spice together. Add half the sifted flour to the egg mixture and fold in gently.

Over a gentle heat melt the copha until warm but not hot. Pour into the flour and egg mixture and beat for 3 minutes. Add the remaining flour and chopped fruit alternately, mixing well with a wooden spoon.

Transfer to the prepared tin, leaving a depression in the centre. Bake for 15 minutes then reduce the heat to 140°C and bake for a further 1½ hours. Test with a skewer before removing from the oven.

Lynette Matchett, Murrumba Downs, QLD

DANISH CHRISTMAS PUDDING

Serves 4–6

This recipe, which I still use, takes me back to the 1950s when I was a young physiotherapist working at a poliomyelitis rehabilitation centre at Hornbeck, Denmark. Many of the Danish patients and staff had gone home for Christmas, so we remaining helped serve the indigenous Greenlander patients their Christmas Eve lunch. The local fishermen had caught a seal, so this, to the delight of the Eskimos, was being served to them, raw.

In the evening we enjoyed a Danish Christmas feast — fruit-stuffed pork, crispy roast potatoes, gherkins and gooseberries followed of course by the traditional Christmas Pudding.

INGREDIENTS

5 cups (1.25 litres) milk
¼ cup (55 g) caster sugar
250 g medium grain rice
1 small wineglass sherry (to your personal taste)
2 teaspoons vanilla essence
½ cup (80 g) blanched and chopped almonds, toasted
250 ml (1 cup) thickened cream, whipped
1 blanched almond, extra
cherry or raspberry sauce, to serve
dash of Kirsch

METHOD

Bring the milk to the boil, and add the sugar and rice. Stir once or twice, lower the heat and simmer, uncovered, for about 25 minutes, until the rice is soft but not mushy. Pour into a shallow bowl to cool quickly then add sherry, vanilla and almonds. Fold the whipped cream into the tepid rice mixture. Drop in the whole blanched 'lucky' almond. Pour into a pretty serving bowl and chill. Serve with cherry or raspberry sauce and a dash of kirsch. Whoever finds the whole almond wins a small prize.

Margaret Fortune, Nambour, QLD

DIS

Serves 12

We don't have a proper name for this recipe — but because when we kids were little we'd say to Mum 'I want some of dis' it has always just been called 'Dis' by the family! My parents make it every Christmas — Dad chops everything, and Mum puts it all together.

INGREDIENTS

55 g brazil nuts

55 g raisins

18 malt or shredded wholewheat biscuits, crushed

15 marshmallows, diced

¼ teaspoon vanilla essence

half a 395 g can condensed milk

shredded coconut

METHOD

Chop the nuts and fruit and combine all the ingredients except the coconut.

Roll in the shredded coconut into log shapes.

Wrap in foil and store in the refrigerator, and cut into slices to serve.

Julie Maree Finnegan, by email

DUCK SALAD
Serves 4

It has taken years, but our family have almost come around to the idea that it isn't necessary to plough through hot turkey with all the trimmings (and all the frazzled temperament that goes with it) at Christmas. But for those of us who think that Christmas isn't Christmas unless there is poultry on the table, even in 40°C heat, this is the perfect compromise! I served it to friends last year and one thought it such a good idea, she has adopted it as her signature salad for hot Christmas days henceforth! It is a light and fresh starter.

INGREDIENTS

1 tablespoon dark soy sauce
2 tablespoons honey
1 teaspoon Chinese five spice, powder
¼ teaspoon white pepper
small knob ginger, finely grated
1 garlic clove, finely chopped
1 small red chilli, finely chopped
4 duck breasts
3 firm yellow nectarines, stoned and quartered
4 tablespoons extra virgin olive oil
150–200 g mixed salad leaves
18 snow peas, julienned
½ red capsicum, julienned
½ red onion, finely sliced
2 oranges, peeled and segmented
juice of ½ orange
freshly ground black pepper

METHOD

Mix the soy sauce, honey and spices. Use to brush the skin side of the breasts and set aside.

Heat an oven grill to 220°C.

Heat a chargrill pan until smoking, toss the nectarines in half the oil and place on the pan until the flesh is charred. Remove from the heat and set aside.

Sear the duck breasts on the hot chargrill pan for about 30 seconds each side. Place onto a rack on a baking tray, skin side up. Place under the grill for 10–12 minutes. When rare, remove to a plate and place under foil to rest.

Slice the duck breasts and toss with salad greens, vegetables and fruit. Arrange on a large shallow serving dish. Mix the orange juice and remaining oil, season with black pepper and dress the salad when ready to serve.

Jo Broderick, Brighton, VIC

GRANDMA GRIBBLE'S CHRISTMAS PUDDING RECIPE

Makes 2 puddings

This recipe creates a lovely light and delicious Christmas pudding, making it very suitable for our hot Christmas weather, and is quite unlike the traditional puddings. It can be served hot (reheated) or cold, with custard, cream or ice cream. The recipe has been handed down from my grandmother, Selina Alice Gribble (1873–1951), through my mother and now I have passed it on to my daughters and daughter-in-law. It has been enjoyed by many and helps to pass on memories of a charming and very busy Australian lady, wife of a country clergyman, and much loved mother of nine children.

INGREDIENTS

¼ loaf white sandwich bread
250 g seeded raisins
250 g sultanas
250 g currants
250 g mixed peel
100 g cherries
200 g plain flour
250 g butter or margarine
250 g soft brown sugar
½ cup (60 g) slivered almonds
juice of ½ a lemon
5 eggs, beaten
¼ cup (60 ml) brandy or sherry
pinch of salt

METHOD

Soak the bread overnight in water. Squeeze out the excess water (bread will then be like pulp). Mix the fruit with a little of the flour. Add the fruit to the bread.

Cream the butter or margarine and sugar in another bowl. Mix this in with the bread and fruit. Add the almonds, lemon juice, eggs and brandy or sherry. Mix in the sifted flour with a pinch of salt.

Grease two 4-cup pudding basins. Line the bottom of each basin with a small piece of baking paper. Divide the mixture evenly between the two basins, and cover with baking paper.

Tie with string around the rim.

Steam the puddings in a saucepan with about 5 cm of water for about 3–4 hours. Check and add more water regularly.

Wendy J. Handes, by email

MACADAMIA SQUARES
Makes 20 squares

This recipe is a favourite for our family at Christmas. Everyone who's ever had it just loves it. Deliciously wicked. Not for the health conscious but once a year is okay. It originates from the north coast of NSW in a macadamia plantation area and came to us via a friend who made it for a Christmas party.

INGREDIENTS

½ cup (70 g) chopped macadamia nuts
1 cup (55g) shredded coconut
75 g butter
250 g white marshmallows
4 cups (120 g) cornflakes
125 g dark chocolate, melted

METHOD:

Line a 20 x 30 cm slice tin with baking paper.

Toast the nuts and coconut in a frying pan or in the oven. Set aside to cool.

Melt the butter in a large saucepan and add the marshmallows. Stir over low heat until melted.

Mix in the nuts, coconut and cornflakes. Press into the tin. Chill until set. Drizzle with the melted chocolate and cut into squares.

Barbara Godfrey, Monash, ACT

MANDATORY SAUCE
Makes 1 jar

So named by my cousin over 30 years ago, who sampled it with ham and prawns at Christmas time. I have made it each Christmas since. It also goes deliciously with turkey or chicken. Add more garblic if you care!

INGREDIENTS
1 can plum jam
½ cup (125 ml) white vinegar
2 finger size pieces fresh ginger, peeled and sliced
6 large garlic cloves, each cut into 3

METHOD
Boil up all of the ingredients for 15 minutes, then leave to let flavours develop for 2–3 hours. Strain into a glass jar and store in the fridge for up to 3 months.

Jeanette Trefle, Red Hill, QLD

Mrs Mirabito's Fruit Cake
Makes 1 cake

For years every Christmas my mother made this fruit cake for the fire brigade men who used to call around to her villa and check the smoke detectors. As she got older she had to use a frying pan to cook the cakes in as they were too heavy for her to lift into the oven.

There is a similar tradition with the local post office girls. In 1994 the Commonwealth Bank closed down in Weipa which created extra work for the girls. Every December I make them the fruit cake for Christmas. These hard working girls really deserve this treat!

Ingredients

450 g mixed dried fruit
1 cup (175 g) sultanas
1 cup (160 g) chopped pitted dates
1 cup (175 g) raisins
1 cup (200 g) brown sugar
1 cup (250 ml) water
225 g butter
1 teaspoon bicarbonate of soda
1 teaspoon mixed spice
2 well beaten eggs
1¼ cups (180 g) self-raising flour, sifted
1 cup (150 g) plain flour, sifted
½ teaspoon vanilla essence
½ cup (125 ml) rum or sherry
½ cup (80 g) blanched almonds

METHOD

Place the fruit, sugar, water, butter, bicarb and mixed spice into a large saucepan. Stir to combine and bring to the boil. Leave overnight to cool.

Preheat the oven to 160°C. Grease and line a cake loaf tin (a loaf tin is most suitable for this).

Add the eggs, sifted flours, vanilla essence and rum or sherry to the fruit mixture. Stir until well combined.

Place the mixture into the prepared tin. Lightly dampen your hand with water and wet the top of the cake. Decorate with the blanched almonds.

Bake on the middle shelf for about 1 hour and 40 minutes. Check at 1 hour and 30 minutes, turn the cake tin around on the oven shelf. Test with a skewer. Leave in the tin until the cake cools. Store in a container in the fridge.

Jan Porter, Weipa, QLD

Mum and Angie's Plum Pudding

Serves 8–10

After Mum died, it took my sister Angela many attempts to reconstruct this recipe as no formal record of weights and measures had been kept. As an old country cook, and mother of 11 kids, mum's cooking was all done by memory. Scoops of this, cups and pinches of that were all thrown into the bowl. We only managed to celebrate one Christmas with 'The Pudding' taking pride of place on the table instead of the turkey, before Angela lost her fight with breast cancer. Before dying Angie made a grand ceremony of passing 'The Pudding Recipe' on to me, making me promise to cook it early Christmas morning just as our mum had always done, and I do. I even put threepences in it! This recipe has never once failed. It's just a no-fuss, very cheap, old-fashioned pudding, full of flavour and memories. It can't be made weeks in advance, just a day or two and kept in aluminium foil or plastic wrap.

Ingredients

2 tablespoons butter
2 cups (300 g) plain flour
2 cups (300 g) self-raising flour
3 teaspoons mixed spice
3 teaspoons ground nutmeg
3 teaspoons ground cinnamon
2 tablespoons sugar
3 cups (525 g) mixed fruit (the cheaper house brands are fine)
375 g raisins
2¾ cups (685 ml) milk
2 tablespoons golden syrup
2½ tablespoons white vinegar
2 teaspoons bicarbonate of soda

METHOD

First prepare the cloth. Soak a pudding cloth or piece of calico in hot water. Spread it out and dust with plain flour. Line a bowl with the cloth to make it easier to fill.

Rub the butter into the flours and spices. Add the sugar and fruit. In a medium saucepan, bring the milk and golden syrup to the boil. Add the vinegar and bicarb and quickly mix together. While still foamy add to the flour mixture and mix together.

Put the mixture into the prepared cloth, gather the ends and tie very tightly with string as close as possible to the mixture. Boil in approximately 5 litres of boiling water with an inverted saucer in the bottom of pot for 4 hours. Remember to keep topping the pot up with boiling water.

David Tickner, Coldstream, VIC

NANA'S SHORTBREAD
Makes 12–16 pieces

Every Christmas, as soon as we arrived at Nana's house and there was a gap in the adult's conversation, invariably one of us kids would pipe up — 'Nana, is there any shortbread?'. Of course, the question was just a formality. It was guaranteed that there would be a tin of pale, buttery shortbread, baked to perfection. Now Aunty Marie continues to bake this recipe, with formidable success. As the recipe is handed down with love, even to our extended family, you can be sure that there will always be a welcoming tin of shortbread wherever we have Christmas.

INGREDIENTS
250 g butter
1 cup (125 g) icing sugar or icing mixture (Marie always uses icing mixture)
2 cups (300 g) plain flour, sifted
1 cup (125 g) rice flour or cornflour, sifted
pinch of salt

METHOD
Preheat the oven to 180°C and lightly grease a baking tray.

Cream the butter and icing sugar. Gradually add in the sifted flours until the mixture comes together to a crumbly consistency (don't overwork it!).

Place onto the prepared tray and press down with your hand. Roll with a glass to smooth the surface. Mark lines on the shortbread for cutting into squares, and prick each square with a fork for decoration.

Bake for 15–20 minutes, on the middle shelf of the oven, until lightly coloured.

Remove from the oven and cut the shortbread into squares while hot but leave on the tray until cool.

Mary Pritchard, Lilyfield, NSW

NANNY'S CHRISTMAS BISCUITS
Makes 50–60

This is a Danish recipe that my mother has made every Christmas for as long as I can remember! She makes hundreds of these little biscuits and puts them in tins for the whole family and her friends. I have only just snavelled the recipe after leaving home 16 years ago — so don't tell her I have told you about it! It is her special treat to us all every Christmas.

INGREDIENTS
    250 g butter
    250 g brown sugar
    250 g golden syrup
    ½ teaspoon bicarbonate of soda
    1½ teaspoons ground cinnamon
    ½ teaspoon ground cardamom
    1 teaspoon ground cloves
    50 ml rose water
    750 g 9 (5 cups) plain flour
    1 egg white, lightly beaten
    almond flakes

METHOD
Melt the butter, sugar and golden syrup without boiling. Cool, then add the bicarb soda. Add the spices and rose water, then the flour. Mix well, until it forms a ball in the bowl. Roll into two sausages (about the thickness of a 50 cent piece). Put into the fridge for a day.

Preheat the oven to 180°C.

Slice the dough thinly, place on trays and brush with the egg white. Put a flake of almond on each biscuit and cook for about 10 minutes.

Sue Hill, Esperance, WA

Oliebollen (Dutch Doughnuts)

Makes 24

I was born in Holland and came to Australia in 1957. The following recipe has been a must for New Year's Eve for as long as I can remember. My father always made them and then, for the last 30 years, I made the mixture and my husband cooked them. My husband died two years ago, and the first New Year's Eve after he died I wasn't going to make them. My daughter told me that she really wanted me to make them as that would keep the tradition alive, and if I didn't feel like it she would take over, as she will take over after I'm gone. Last New Year's Eve was so hot here in Adelaide, 43°C, that I made them on New Year's Day.

Ingredients

1 kg self-raising flour
1 tablespoon salt
25 g dry yeast
200 g sultanas
200 g currants
2 Granny Smith apples, peeled and grated (or finely chopped)
grated rind of 1 lemon (optional)
3 large eggs, lightly beaten
4 cups (1 litre) milk
4 cups (1 litre) hot water
vegetable oil, for deep frying
icing sugar, to dust

METHOD

Sift the flour into a large bowl. Add the salt and yeast and mix through the flour. Add the fruit and rind; mix until evenly combined. Make a well in the centre and pour in the eggs and half the combined milk and water.

Mix well with a wooden spoon. Slowly add the remaining milk and water until the mixture drops off the back of a spoon. Cover the bowl with a tea towel and let the mixture rise until doubled in size (I leave it for about 4 hours).

Once again mix with a wooden spoon and leave for another hour. Heat the oil to 180°C in a large saucepan.

Using an ice-cream scoop, drop spoonfuls of the mixture into the hot oil. Cook until nicely browned. They will turn half way. Drain on paper towels, and serve hot or cold covered with sifted icing sugar.

Joanne Kegel, Surrey Downs, SA

Pullao (flavoured yellow rice)

Serves 6

This is a wonderful way of preparing rice and was traditionally served at Christmas when I was a child. It is a Goan recipe and has been influenced by Portuguese and Indian cuisine. It is also a healthy dish as it contains turmeric, an ingredient used over the centuries to help prevent many diseases.

Ingredients

1 cup (200 g) basmati rice
1 tablespoon light olive, sunflower or vegetable oil
1 onion, chopped
2 cardamom pods
2 cinnamon sticks
4 whole cloves
A little less than 1 teaspoon ground turmeric
2 cups (500 ml) chicken stock
salt to taste

Method

Wash the rice about 3 times in cold water, drain and set aside. Heat the oil and fry the onion over medium heat until opaque (don't let it brown).

Add the cardamom, cinnamon and cloves and fry for a couple of minutes, stirring continuously with a wooden spoon. Lower the heat to medium–low and add the turmeric and fry for a minute, stirring.

Add the washed rice (watch out for the rising steam which can burn your hands) and fry for a minute or so, gently stirring so that it doesn't stick to the pan.

Add the stock and stir gently to ensure no rice is stuck to the bottom of the pan. Add a little salt if desired (although stock usually has enough salt) at this stage and stir.

Increase the heat to medium–high or until it is bubbling (not boiling). Put the lid on. Check every couple of minutes or so to see if the water level has reduced. Stir each time you lift the lid to ensure the rice is not sticking to the bottom. The consistency should be that of runny porridge (there should be some water left around the grains but it shouldn't be as watery as a soup). From my experience this takes a bit of trial and error to get it right.

When there is sufficient water left around the grains, put the lid back on and DO NOT OPEN AGAIN until done (this keeps all the remaining steam inside the pan to cook the rice). IMMEDIATELY reduce the heat to the lowest setting, (so that the heat is just on). Set the clock for 15 minutes. (Though sometimes the rice can be cooked in 12 minutes depending on how much moisture was left in pan.)

When 15 minutes is up, IMMEDIATELY remove the pan from the heat and set aside. Remove the lid and with a flat wooden spoon gently bring the rice at the bottom of the pan to the top as the rice is still cooking with the heat in the pan. Taste the rice and, if it is still not done, you may have to sprinkle a little warm water and put the pan back on a VERY LOW heat for a minute or so with the lid on.

Susana Smith, by email

Rina's Kul-Kuls
Makes approximately 50

Kul-kul making is an age old Anglo-Indian tradition that even Ghandi couldn't get rid of. It's usually a day long process, a compulsory entry in your busy pre-Christmas diary. A day where the family gather around the kitchen table, armed with forks. From new generations in highchairs to older generations in wheelchairs, no one escapes the Kul-kul making day. Christmas goodwill and carols with Bing and Dean complete the setting.

In our family the traditional making of the dough and frosting is passed down the female line, and the frying down the male line. The final eating makes it all worthwhile.

INGREDIENTS

1 tin coconut milk
4 tablespoons ghee
4 free-range duck eggs
6 tablespoons sugar
250 g self-raising flour
250 g plain flour
vegetable oil for deep frying

Frosting
6 tablespoons sugar
water

METHOD

Place the coconut milk in the fridge the night before to separate the cream on top.

Melt the ghee and allow to cool.

Combine the eggs and sugar and beat with vigour. Sift the flours together. Add the ghee to the egg mixture. Using a rice server and Herculean strength, gradually fold the flour into the liquid mixture and make into a soft dough with the thick cream from the coconut milk. (The 2008 amendment will trial the bread maker for the dough making!)

Once the family have assembled, roll the dough into balls the size of a marble. Flatten the ball onto the back of a floured fork and roll off towards the tip making a curl (this is the time-consuming process made easier by many hands).

Deep fry in the oil until golden brown. Allow to cool, then commence frosting the Kul–kuls.

To make the frosting, moisten the sugar with a small amount of water. Dissolve over low heat, until bubbling. Quickly dunk the Kul–kuls in and out of the bubbling mixture. Allow to dry on baking paper. Store in an airtight container and (try to) hide away until Christmas Day.

Sheryl Townsend, Freshwater Creek, VIC

Roasted Nectarines
Serves 6

This recipe came about one Christmas when I had an overabundance of ripe nectarines in the fridge. These are fabulous with roast pork, turkey or chicken. My family like them with anything for any occasion. Of course it has to be when nectarines are in season, but that is summer and party time for most folks.

Ingredients

9 nectarines
2 tablespoons white balsamic vinegar
¼ cup (60 ml) maple syrup
30 g butter
6 slices prosciutto

Method

Preheat the oven to 180°C. Grease a small baking dish, or line with baking paper (much easier to wash up).

Halve the nectarines, then quarter them and arrange in the baking dish. Sprinkle with the balsamic vinegar and maple syrup. Dot with the butter. Roast for 10–15 minutes.

Meanwhile chop the prosciutto and fry in a pan until crisp; set aside.

To serve, spoon the nectarines on to individual plates or a serving platter and sprinkle with the crispy prosciutto.

Note: I have also used this recipe as an entrée by serving the nectarines and prosciutto on a bed of baby spinach. Add a sprinkling of good feta cheese and a little fresh thyme. Toasted pine nuts are also a great addition, but are not always affordable.

Yellow nectarines are best because they tend to have a slightly more tart flavour, but white will work. They halve quite easily if you cut them first and give them a little twist.

Vickie McEnery, by email

Sago Plum Puddding
Serves 8

One Christmas over fifty years ago, as a young bride, I decided to impress my family who were expected for Christmas dinner. I decided to make the traditional pudding, full of all kinds of dried fruit, and boiled for many hours in 'a cloth'. I agonised for days before I finally had enough courage to try out the recipe (from an old book which once belonged to my grandmother). To my surprise it turned out beautifully. The recipe stated that it had to 'mature' and hang in an airy place. After consulting my husband we decided that the best place to hang it would be in the air passage in the dairy (we were dairy farmers). Each day as I passed by I would check to see that my pudding was safe. Eventually Christmas Day arrived and I spent the early hours preparing a traditional Christmas dinner of ham and duckling for the family, who were due to arrive mid–morning. Hubby was sent out to cut down the 'pudding' and he reluctantly returned with my creation. Imagine my despair and horror when I discovered that a small mouse hole had appeared and the entire contents had been nibbled out!!! Trying to save face a very hurried 'Sago Plum Pudding' was whipped up and served in place of my masterpiece.

Ingredients
½ cup (100 g) sago
1 cup (250 ml) milk
125 g butter, melted
1 cup (80 g) fresh breadcrumbs
1 cup (175 g) raisins
¾ cup (150 g) brown sugar
1 tablespoon finely chopped ginger
2 teaspoons bicarbonate of soda

METHOD

Soak the sago in the milk overnight.

Next morning melt the butter, and stir into breadcrumbs. Add the raisins, sugar, ginger and bicarbonate of soda, and mix well. If the mixture appears not slack enough then a little more milk can be added. Put into a greased pudding basin, cover and stand the basin in a saucepan of water and boil for 3 hours.

This is especially good served hot with homemade boiled custard and whipped cream on top. Some people prefer ice cream.

Coral Whiting, Henty, NSW

Sardelle in 'Savor' (Sardines Marinated in Vinegar)

Serves 4

My family is from Trieste (near Venice) in north–eastern Italy and used to make this dish on Christmas Eve, which in some parts of Europe, is a bigger celebration than Christmas Day. In this part of Italy, fish is the main meal. This dish is served as an entrée.

Ingredients

500 g sardines (not tiny ones)
3 tablespoons olive oil
2 medium onions, finely sliced
2 bay leaves
salt and pepper
¾ cup (185 ml) red wine vinegar
flour
additional olive oil, for frying

Method

Remove the heads and internal parts of the sardines — wash and drain. Heat the oil and cook the onions over medium heat with the bay leaves, until golden but not brown. Season with salt and pepper to taste.

Add the vinegar and cook for a few minutes. Remove from the stove and leave to cool. Coat the sardines with the flour (to which a little salt has been added) and fry in the additional oil until cooked. Drain on paper towel and add a little salt.

When cooled, put one layer of sardines into a ceramic dish and top with some of the onion mixture, then repeat the layers. Refrigerate for one day so that the flavours mix and intensify. Serve cold or at room temperature.

Ambra Sancin, Surry Hills, NSW

SPICED BEEF

Serves 8

This is a very popular Irish recipe which my mother obtained from The New World Radiation *(a gas cooker of the day)* Cookery Book *(1935 edition). As a child I used to sit on the cooking table and watch this cheap piece of meat be transformed into the most delicious Christmas dinner dish. I carried this recipe with me to Australia. It took me two years in Australia to twig that a refrigerator was essential in 'spicing' the brisket.*

INGREDIENTS

1.5 kg brisket (meat should have some fat streaks)
1 cup (300 g) coarse salt
¼ (50 g) brown sugar
½ teaspoon allspice
½ teaspoon ground nutmeg
1½ teaspoons ground cloves
¼ teaspoon dried thyme
freshly ground pepper
½ teaspoon ground bay leaves
1 teaspoon sweet pineapple powder (ask your butcher)
50 g black treacle or golden syrup

METHOD

Rub the meat with the salt and leave overnight in the fridge.

Combine the sugar, allspice, nutmeg, cloves, thyme, pepper, bay leaves and sweet pineapple powder. Rub the salt off the meat and wipe dry. Rub the meat with the spice mixture, cover and put in the fridge for 2 days.

Heat the treacle and pour over the meat. Place into a plastic bag and keep in the fridge for a week. During that time every day push the meat around in its plastic bag.

Remove from the fridge, roll and tie the meat with string. Place into a large saucepan and cover with cold water. Cook gently for 2 hours. Leave to cool in the saucepan water.

Serve hot or cold over the Christmas festivities.

Barry O'Keeffe, Wembley Downs, WA

SPICY CORIANDER HUMMUS

Serves 8

This recipe was created for a family get together, and now it is just expected to be brought to all functions that are held by my rather large family. I am one of ten siblings and our family Christmas, usually held in mid-December, has up to sixty immediate relations. Most of my brothers and sisters are married and there are over forty grand- and great-grandchildren.

INGREDIENTS

400 g can chickpeas
1 tablespoon tahini (sesame paste)
Juice of 1 lemon
2 large heaped teaspoons each ground cumin and ground coriander
½ teaspoon crushed chilli paste (sambal oelek)
lots of freshly crushed garlic — up to 6 cloves (this gives it a bite)
fresh coriander leaves (I like to put about ¾ of the bunch)
olive oil

METHOD

Put all the ingredients except the oil into a blender or food processor. With the motor running, add the oil in a thin stream — you can decide on how thick you want it to be.

Best served with warm Turkish bread.

Margaret Teresa Burke, by email

TURKISH DELIGHT AND CHOCOLATE FRIDGE DESSERT

Serves 12

Quick and easy to make when you have guests galore hanging over the table either Christmas Day or Boxing Day. With an average of thirty guests each Boxing Day, after a heavy Christmas day in the food area, this recipe is a winner. A best friend passed it on to me, and I would be lost without it — great standby. Try it for yourself.

INGREDIENTS

400 g good quality chocolate, coarsely chopped
1 cup (250 ml) thickened cream
2 tablespoons Cointreau (small sample bottles are great)
250 g Marie biscuits, coarsely chopped
6 x 55 g chocolate covered Turkish Delight, quartered
1 cup (140 g) pistachio nuts or unsalted cashews
170 g Craisins (dried cranberries)
icing sugar, to dust
double cream, to serve

METHOD

Line the base of a 20 cm (base measurement) springform tin with baking paper.

Place the chocolate and cream into a large saucepan over low heat. Cook, stirring, for 5 minutes or until the chocolate melts and the mixture is smooth. Remove from the heat. Stir in the Cointreau and set aside for 5 minutes to cool.

Combine the biscuits, Turkish delight, pistachios or cashews and Craisins in a large bowl. Add the chocolate mixture and stir until well combined. Spoon into the prepared tin, pressing firmly to fit. Place in the fridge for 6 hours or until firm. Dust with icing sugar and cut into slices. Divide among serving plates and serve with cream, if desired.

Susan Chadwick, Maryborough, QLD

WILSON SISTERS' PUMPKIN SALAD

Serves 6–8

Have you ever eaten Christmas dinner within sight of the sea? My lucky family has done so since I was a child. Being close to the beach adds a layer of welcome informality and several years ago our traditional Christmas dinner was replaced by a combination of roasted meats and contemporary salads. This dish started life in a food magazine but it has been adapted so much by we five sisters that there are few aspects in common with the original. Despite the changing nature of the Christmas menu, this has become a permanent inclusion. Because it's delicious!

INGREDIENTS

pumpkin, diced into 2–3 cm pieces
olive oil
1 red onion
large handful of snow peas
enough rocket to spread over a large platter
feta cheese
walnuts or toasted pine nuts (optional)
balsamic vinegar
½–1 teaspoon pomegranate molasses, optional

Method

Toss the pumpkin in olive oil and roast the pumpkin until brown and tender. While the pumpkin is roasting, thinly slice the onion. Blanch the snow peas and shred finely into julienne strips. They should be crunchy. Crumble the feta.

When the pumpkin is cooked, combine the onion and pumpkin while hot.

Arrange the rocket on a platter, and scatter the snow peas over. When the pumpkin mixture is cooled to room temperature, place on top of the snow peas.

Scatter the feta and nuts (if included) on top.

Dress the salad lightly — the balsamic vinegar should not overwhelm the other flavours. The pomegranate molasses provides a touch of sweetness. Fresh pomegranate would also provide great colour, flavour and texture.

Note: The quantities are elastic — use enough to serve your crowd.

Jill Wilson, Footscray, VIC

AUSTRALIA DAY

Aussie Tiramisu

Serves 8–10

Digging a hole in the backyard and cooking tea in the ashes can be fun with the grandchildren but it is not my idea of native cuisine.

Everyone comments on the way Australian cuisine has expanded over the last few decades. We have had the European influence, then the Asian. Now our chefs are looking for new challenges and native cuisine has a lot to offer.

What I like doing is modifying some favourite recipes. This can be as simple as adding wattleseed or lemon myrtle to shortbread biscuits or muntries to an impossible pie.

You all have your favourite recipes, why not try substituting a native herb?

Ingredients

Australian Honey Liqueur
350 ml Australian Honey (leather wood, blue gum, red mahogany or yellow box)
700 ml vodka (or other unflavoured white spirit)

2 tablespoons wattleseed
1¼ cups (310 ml) water
½ cup (125 ml) thickened cream
⅓ cup (40 g) icing sugar
2 cups (500 g) mascarpone cheese
250 g packet sponge finger biscuits (savoiardi)
wattleseed or lemon myrtle, to sprinkle
wild rosella flowers or strawberries, to decorate

METHOD

To make the Australian honey liqueur pour the honey into a 1 litre container. Add the vodka and shake to dissolve the honey. This may take some time so leave it in a handy spot and shake as often as you can over a couple of days. Once the honey is dissolved put in a dark cupboard for at least 6 weeks. Rack off. The lees are okay to use in the tiramisu when fresh.

Boil the wattleseed in the water for about 2 minutes and put aside to cool.

Beat the cream and icing sugar in a small bowl until soft peaks form, fold in the mascarpone. Carefully stir ⅓ cup (80 ml) honey liqueur through the mixture. Mix ⅔ cup (170 ml) honey liqueur with the cooled wattleseed water.

Dip half the biscuits one at a time in the wattleseed honey liqueur mixture and arrange them in a single layer in a 2.5 litre (10 cup) glass dish. Spread half (or a little less, depending on the shape of your dish) of the cream mixture over the biscuits in the dish.

Dip the remaining biscuits in the wattleseed mixture and arrange on top of the cream layer. Spread the remaining cream mixture over the top. Sprinkle with wattleseed or lemon myrtle if it blends well with your honey liqueur. Cover and refrigerate for at least several hours. Best made the day before.

Decorate with wild rosella flowers for a real statement, alternatively strawberries are very acceptable.

R S Cooper, Coles Bay, TAS

Australia Day Mixed Lamb Grill

Serves 10

Ingredients

Spiced Lamb Rissoles
(makes about 10)
500 g lamb mince
3 spring onions, finely chopped
1 garlic clove, crushed
1 teaspoon each ground white pepper, ground cinnamon, ground
    cumin, salt, ground cloves, ground coriander and paprika

Minty Chops
1 cup (250 ml) extra virgin olive oil
1 cup (250 ml) white wine vinegar
½ cup chopped fresh mint
1 garlic clove, crushed
1 large teaspoon honey
salt and pepper
10–12 lamb chops

Red Rumps
2 lamb rump, about 300 g each
1 cup (250 ml) red wine
1 cup (250 ml) extra virgin olive oil
2 garlic cloves, crushed
handful fresh rosemary, leaves stripped from stalk and roughly
    chopped
salt and freshly ground black pepper

Method

To make the spiced lamb rissoles, knead all the ingredients together until thoroughly combined. With wet hands, roll tablespoons of mixture into balls and flatten slightly.

To make the minty chops mix everything together except for the chops. Pour over the chops and leave to marinate for at least 1 hour before cooking, but preferably overnight in the fridge.

To make the red rumps, combine all together and marinate in the fridge overnight.

These are all cooked on the barbecue. Cook the rumps first until pink, then lift, wrap in foil, and rest while you cook the chops and rissoles. Slice the rumps thinly and put all the meat on a large platter to serve, scattered with extra fresh herbs.

Susan Cole, North Perth, WA

BARBECUED ANTIPASTO SKEWERS
Serves 6

Jenny and the children share my love of food. As well as having adventurous tastebuds, we enjoy the creativity of presenting food. This recipe grew out of the melting pot of our Australian and Italian heritages.

INGREDIENTS
2 Italian semi-dried sausages
26 pitted kalamata olives
handful of basil leaves, torn
havarti or provolone cheese, chopped
4 slices chargrilled eggplant, chopped
2 Roma tomatoes, chopped
2 marinated artichoke hearts, chopped
1 red capsicum, chopped

METHOD
Slice the sausages into 52 thin diagonal slices. Cut 13 thin bamboo skewers in half, cutting on an angle to make a point (half of them will have 2 points).

Take a piece of sausage, and wrap an olive with a piece of basil and cheese. Thread onto the skewer lengthways (through the ends of the sausage).

Repeat with another piece of sausage, and add a couple of other ingredients this time. Repeat using different combinations of ingredients. The children love to help, especially choosing the combinations.

Place onto the barbecue for a couple of minutes to brown the sausage and get the cheese to run. Serve on a white platter. The colours, aromas and flavours are a wonderful way to start a barbecue with family or friends.

Martyn Scott Cavanagh, by email

BARBECUED FILLET OF KANGAROO

Serves 2

Since experiencing a heart attack in 2002, my switch to kangaroo meat was one of several lifestyle changes I made. This has reduced my cholesterol level and has meant a healthier and hopefully longer life for my family and myself. You too can improve your lifestyle, probably increase your life expectancy and contribute to a healthier rural landscape — eat more 'roo. The 2007 Australian of the year Dr Tim Flannery is an advocate of eating kangaroo meat. Kangaroos can be harvested in a sustainable manner. They have soft pads on their feet which have much less impact on our landscape than hard-hoofed stock such as cattle and sheep which can damage our topsoil, which contributes to the dust storms we experience during inland drought. Our larger stores and specialty butchers are now stocking kangaroo meat and the more product we purchase, the more valued the animal becomes and more farmers will be prepared to manage their properties, at least in part, for kangaroos.

P.S. I have no association with the kangaroo harvesting industry.

INGREDIENTS

Marinade
1 tablespoon vegetable oil
2 teaspoons sherry
2 tablespoons seeded mustard
1 garlic clove, finely chopped
1 drop of sesame oil
good dash of freshly ground pepper

500 g kangaroo fillet

Method

Thoroughly mix the marinade ingredients (I suggest placing all ingredients in a screw cap bottle and shaking vigorously into a slurry).

Coat the fillet steak with the marinade in a sealable container and refrigerate for several hours or overnight.

Fire up the barbie (enjoy a stubby if you must!), bring the meat to room temperature and make sure the barbecue plate is hot. Have a clock nearby as precise timing is required. Cook the meat for 2 minutes each side for thinner pieces, 3 minutes for thicker pieces, each time spooning over remaining marinade.

Remove the meat from the barbecue plate, place onto a rack and cover with foil, let it stand for 10 minutes. Serve with salad, barbecued or steamed vegies and a glass of good Aussie red wine. One must be prepared to eat this meat rare as kangaroo meat has almost no fat and so overcooking the meat results in tough, leathery meat which is hardly edible. Kangaroo meat is the healthiest red meat available with almost no cholesterol or fat.

Bob Moffatt, Alstonville, NSW

DAMPER
Makes 1 loaf

This is a simple bread, made by hand and baked on the coals of the camp fire. Indigenous Australians made it for centuries, using flour ground from native wild seeds. It became a staple for bushmen and early settlers as all the ingredients were dry (flour, salt, baking powder) and light to carry. Like many of today's convenience foods, you add water and bake.

One school of thought suggests that the name originated because you needed to 'dampen' the fire (reduce the heat) before baking.

INGREDIENTS

2 cups (300 g) self-raising flour
1 teaspoon sugar
½ teaspoon salt
1 teaspoon butter
1½ cups (375 ml) milk (or water)

METHOD

Sift the flour, sugar and salt into a bowl and then add the butter. Add enough milk to make a manageable dough. Shape into a flat ball and place on a greased and floured oven tray, bake at 220°C for 25–30 minutes. Brush with the milk during cooking. When it's done, it should have a browned crust, and sound hollow if you tap with your fingers.

Note: If self-raising flour is not available, add 2 teaspoons of baking powder to 1 cup plain flour.

Myrto Aretakis, Bulleen, VIC

EMU STEAKS WITH PEPPERBERRY AND ROSELLA SAUCE

Serves 2

When trying to devise an Australian dish for the theme Taste of Terroir I assumed most people would go for the kangaroo. I decided to lean towards the other side of the coat of arms and try to cook emu. It was a scary challenge because I know emu can be tough if not cooked correctly but I paired it up with the sweetness of rosella and the complex heat of Tassie pepperberries.

INGREDIENTS

Marinade
3 tablespoons balsamic vinegar
1 teaspoon Dijon mustard
3 tablespoons olive oil
5 dried pepperberries, roughly chopped
3 garlic cloves, crushed

400 g emu fillets

Sauce
8 dried pepperberries
2 tablespoons rosella jam
1 cup (250 ml) white wine

METHOD

To make the marinade, whisk the balsamic vinegar, mustard and olive oil together. Add the pepperberries and garlic and whisk well. Pour the marinade over the meat and toss to combine. Marinate for 3 hours.

To make the sauce, drain the marinade and reserve. Combine the pepperberries and the reserved marinade in a frying pan and cook over low heat to soften the garlic.

Add the rosella jam and the white wine and bring to the boil, melting the jam. Stir the sauce continually so it doesn't stick to the pan. Squash the pepperberries a little so they release their colour and flavour. Remove from the heat.

Cook the emu fillets on a grill or barbecue for a maximum of 2 minutes on each side. Emu meat should be served rare since it's very low in fat and overcooking makes it very tough.

Serve drizzled with the sauce.

Anna Fedeles, Newtown, NSW

GRANDMA'S SPICY TOMATO SAUCE

Makes 6–7 litres

Grandma's Spicy Tomato Sauce is an Australian culinary icon. We use this sauce on all occasions, but especially on our Australia Day Barbie. This recipe has been made every summer by our family for four generations. My grandmother worked as a cook at Yulecart Station, in the western district of Victoria, in the late 1890s. While there she was introduced to this sauce. She continued to make it throughout her life. It became a family favourite and the recipe was handed on to her six daughters. Today it is made by both her grandchildren and great grandchildren.

INGREDIENTS
6 kg tomatoes
5.5 kg apples
500 g onions
30 g whole cloves
500 g salt
1 kg sugar
30 g ground ginger
30 g allspice
1 teaspoon cayenne pepper
5 cups (1.2 litres) vinegar

METHOD
Slice the tomatoes, apples and onions. Put the cloves into a calico or muslin bag and boil together with the other ingredients for 3 hours. Strain, and pour into sterilised bottles while still warm.

Paula Smith, Ballarat, VIC

GWEN'S COLESLAW
Serves 8–10

This recipe was given to me twenty-five years ago by a very dear friend. The recipe was handed down to Janet from her mother, Gwen. I have only given the recipe to a couple of close friends, so I asked Janet for permission to enter this in 'Homecooked Feasts'. She was thrilled that I thought highly enough of it to enter it in the competition. It is very refreshing and I have not met one person who does not like it after tasting it. Provided it is not all eaten when first served, it does actually keep very well.

INGREDIENTS
1 cabbage
2 onions
1 green capsicum
¾ cup (165g) sugar
1 cup (250 ml) white vinegar
¾ cup (185 ml) salad oil
1 teaspoon celery seeds
1 teaspoon dry mustard
salt and pepper

METHOD
Shred the cabbage finely and chop the onions and capsicum. Place the cabbage into a bowl, then the onion and finally the capsicum. Sprinkle the sugar over the mixture. DO NOT STIR.

Boil together the vinegar, oil, celery seeds, dry mustard, salt and pepper. Cool slightly and pour over the cabbage mixture. DO NOT STIR. Refrigerate overnight. Mix together before serving. Will keep for 2 weeks.

Pamela Miller, Hampton, VIC

Hot Potato Salad
Serves 8

This recipe was given to me by a friend, who has since died, who was a wonderful cook. Every time I served this dish everyone wanted the recipe. They used it, passed it on, and always raved about the result. It is a versatile favourite to accompany so many dishes, in summer, winter or any time.

Ingredients

6 medium potatoes, cooked in jackets and diced
    (leave on potato skins)
3 celery stalks, chopped
6 spring onions, chopped
⅓–½ cup mayonnaise (or use
    half mayonnaise and half sour cream)
salt
2–3 hard-boiled eggs, chopped
1 tablespoon mint or flat-leaf parsley
2–3 bacon rashers, chopped
1 cup (125 g) grated cheese

Method

Preheat the oven to 150°C.

Combine the potatoes, celery and spring onion in a large bowl. Toss lightly with the mayonnaise and salt. Gently stir through the egg and mint or parsley and put into a greased ovenproof dish. Lightly cook the bacon in a nonstick frying pan and pour the bacon fat over the potato mixture.

Top with the cheese and bacon, and bake for 20–30 minutes or until the cheese has melted and browned.

You can vary this recipe to your own taste — more celery, onion, eggs, mayonnaise, etc. Once you know it well you won't measure anything.

This is delicious even lukewarm, served with a green salad and barbecued meats. It is also a tasty accompaniment to casseroles.

Note: You can leave out the bacon fat if you want.

Helen Kaye-Smith, by email

JILL'S SEAFOOD CHOWDER
Serves 4

Having to provide 'something Australian' for an Australia Day lunch with friends one year, I put together the following recipe. It has always proved very popular ever since.

INGREDIENTS

1 tablespoon butter
2 bacon rashers, chopped
2 celery stalks, chopped
2 medium onions, chopped
310 g can creamed corn
1 cup (100 g) full cream powdered milk
3 cups (750 ml) water
pepper to taste
seafood of your choice (prawns, firm fleshed fish, oysters, mussels or calamari)

METHOD

Melt the butter in a large saucepan. Add the bacon, celery and onion. Sauté for a few minutes until the onion softens. Add the creamed corn and powdered milk, then add the water gradually, stirring well. (I find it best to mix the powdered milk and water together in a bowl then add to the mixture). Add the pepper. Bring to the boil, lower the heat and simmer for 2 minutes.

Add the seafood and continue to simmer for 2 more minutes. Serve with crusty bread. (In very hot weather allow to cool before serving). Recipe will freeze.

Jill Smith, by email

Joy's Romesco Sauce
Makes 1½ cups

Joy is one of the wonderful parents I met when my eldest daughter Arabella started kindy last year. She is a true 'foodie'. Joy often spoils me with some delicious treat she has created but her Romesco Sauce is my absolute favourite. Since she so happily parted with her recipe it has become a permanent fixture in our fridge. It goes with so many things. Great with barbecued or grilled meat, chicken, fish or prawns. It adds amazing flavour in a sandwich but my 18-month-old daughter Chiara prefers it straight off the spoon, chilli and all!!!

Ingredients

4 garlic cloves, unpeeled
1 Roma tomato, halved and deseeded
2 long red chillies
2 tablespoons whole blanched almonds

2 tablespoons hazelnuts
60 g roasted red capsicums in oil
1 tablespoon red wine vinegar
2 tablespoons water
1 cup (250 ml) olive oil
1 teaspoon salt

Method

Preheat the oven to 180°C.

Wrap the garlic cloves in foil with the tomato and chillies, and bake for 12 minutes. Spread the almonds and hazelnuts on a baking tray and bake for 3–5 minutes. Leave to cool for 15 minutes. This part can be done in advance.

Transfer the almonds and hazelnuts to a food processor (or blender) and blend until finely ground. Squeeze out the garlic and scrape the tomato flesh into the blender, discarding the skins. Split the chillies and remove the seeds, scrape the flesh into the blender, discarding the skin. Roughly chop the capsicums then add to the blender with the vinegar and water. Blitz in the processor. With the motor running, slowly pour in the oil. Season with salt.

Lisa Hammond, Coogee, NSW

LAMB MINCE HAMBURGER PATTY
Serves 4

This is a simple burger patty which has been in our family's recipes for a few generations. Always makes a delicious, flavoursome burger patty, absolutely wonderful for any Australia Day barbecue.

INGREDIENTS
a little oil, for frying
1 onion, finely chopped
2 garlic cloves, crushed
450 g lamb mince
¼ cup (80 g) mint jelly
hamburger buns, to serve
picked cucumber, to serve
yoghurt or mint sauce to serve

METHOD
Heat the oil in a frying pan and cook the onion and garlic until soft and lightly golden; drain on paper towel. Combine the mince, mint jelly, onion and garlic in a bowl. Mix thoroughly, and using damp hands shape into patties.

Fry the patties until browned and cooked through. Place on a bun, with pickled cucumber and a spoonful of yoghurt or mint sauce.

Bronwyn Laracy, by email

LASHBACK QUINOA SALAD
Serves 6–8

This recipe is perfect as a lunch, in a picnic hamper or as an accompaniment to a barbecue. Quinoa is a seed-like grain from South America and is a perfect protein. It can be purchased in health food stores and some supermarkets. My dislike of Sam Kekovich's lamb advertisements inspired this vegetarian recipe. Instead of lamb on Australia Day I was inspired to take my Quinoa Salad with vegetarian sausages to an Australia Day barbecue. It was loved by vegetarians and non-vegetarians alike! Don' t forget the vegetarians!

INGREDIENTS
1 kg Jap pumpkin, chopped
olive oil
salt
1 cup (125 g) pumpkin seeds (pepitas)
1 cup (200 g) quinoa
2½ cups (625 ml) water or vegetable stock
1 eggplant, finely diced
1 capsicum, diced
1 Lebanese cucumber, diced
1 punnet cherry tomatoes
1 cup chopped, flat-leaf parsley
1 cup linseeds

METHOD

Preheat the oven to 180°C.

Place the pumpkin onto an oven tray, drizzle with a little olive oil and sprinkle with salt (if desired). Bake until tender and brown. Toast the pumpkin seeds by tossing in oil (and salt if desired) and baking for 7–8 minutes. Cool.

Pour the quinoa into a microwave-safe bowl. Pour in the water or stock. Microwave on high for 15 minutes, stirring once. The water should be absorbed and the quinoa soft.

Heat a little olive oil in a frying pan and cook the eggplant until crisp (it adds a great texture to the salad).

Add all the ingredients to the cooled quinoa and toss the salad together before serving.

Natalie McKenna, East Melbourne, VIC

Prawns with Boab

Serves 4–6

The boab is unique in that it is only found in the Kimberley Region of Western Australia, and has become an icon for the area. It is an exciting new bush food taste sensation. Both tubers and young leaves of the baby boab can be eaten. The texture of the boab tuber is similar to water chestnuts. They are crisp and white with a sweet delicate nutty flavour. The leaves are rich in Vitamins A and C.

Ingredients

Marinade
1 egg white
1 teaspoon sesame oil
2 teaspoons cornflour
sea salt and freshly ground white pepper

450 g green prawns, peeled and deveined
2 tablespoons salt
450 ml peanut oil
1½ tablespoons finely chopped fresh ginger
1 tablespoon chopped garlic
½ small onion, thinly sliced
1 cup (x g) sliced boab
1 cup (150 g) peas, cooked
1 tablespoon sherry
½ teaspoon sugar
1 teaspoon salt
2 teaspoons sesame oil
2 tablespoons finely chopped spring onions
freshly ground white pepper

Method

Wash the prawns in cold water with the salt. Rinse well and pat dry. Combine with all the marinade ingredients, mix well and leave covered in the fridge for 20 minutes.

Heat a wok and add the oil, reserving 1 tablespoon. When very hot, remove from the heat and add the prawns. Cook, stirring vigorously to prevent sticking, until the prawns turn pink. Drain on paper towels, and discard the oil.

Wipe the wok clean and reheat with the reserved oil. Add the ginger and garlic, and stir fry for 10 seconds. Add the onion and stir fry for 2 minutes.

Return the prawns to the wok. Add the boab, peas, sherry, sugar and salt. Stir fry the mixture for 3 minutes, then stir in the sesame oil and garnish with the spring onion. Season with white pepper.

Dulcie Hewitt, WA

ROBIN'S NANA'S SALAD
Serves 4–6

My grandmother was born at Inglewood in country Victoria in 1900. This is her recipe and I believe it was handed down from her mother. It reminds me of lazy summer days gone by, happy family gatherings and old fashioned cold cooked meats. It is a very easy recipe.

INGREDIENTS
    1 large iceberg lettuce, finely sliced
    1 medium white onion, finely grated
    4 eggs, hard boiled
    2 rounded teaspoons mustard powder
    2 tablespoons white sugar
    ½ cup (125 ml) white vinegar
    ½–⅔ cup cream
    salt and pepper

METHOD
Place the lettuce and onion into a salad bowl. Cover with plastic wrap and refrigerate overnight.

Shell the hard-boiled eggs. Peel the whites from the yolks. Slice the whites and put aside. Place the yolks in a small bowl and crush together with the mustard and sugar. Slowly add the vinegar, mixing well. Drizzle in the cream slowly then add the sliced egg whites. Season to taste. You may need to add more vinegar, mustard, cream or sugar depending on individual preference. Cover this mixture with plastic wrap and refrigerate overnight.

Just before serving, add the egg mixture to the lettuce and onion, but no more than 10 minutes ahead as it does not present well if kept too long.

Robin White, Hobart, TAS

Shredded Chicken and Cabbage Salad
Serves 6

I am a retired IT consultant. Cooking is my hobby and I have written an entire Vietnamese cookbook but cannot afford to print it. This is a recipe from my book. This one is wonderful as a summer treat, and it's healthy too.

Ingredients

1 medium carrot, grated
1 medium onion, sliced
1 tablespoon vinegar
2 tablespoons sugar
½ small cabbage (about 500 g), shredded
1 tablespoon fish sauce
2 garlic cloves, crushed
1 teaspoon sugar, extra
2 skinless chicken breast fillets
2 tablespoons vegetable oil
1 cup (250 ml) oil, extra
1 packet prawn crackers
roughly chopped basil, Vietnamese mint or coriander
1 tablespoon fried shallot flakes (optional)

Sauce
3 tablespoons lemon juice or vinegar
2 heaped tablespoons sugar
3 tablespoons fish sauce
1 chopped chilli (optional)

Method

Combine all the sauce ingredients and stir well.

Combine the carrot, onion, vinegar and 1 tablespoon sugar in a plastic container or bowl, and set aside for 10 minutes. Drain off the liquid.

Place the cabbage into a large bowl and sprinkle with the remaining 1 tablespoon sugar. Stand for 10 minutes, then squeeze out all excess water.

Combine the fish sauce, crushed garlic and extra sugar. Use to coat the chicken.

Heat a nonstick frying pan until it is very hot. Add the oil and reduce the heat to medium. Shallow fry the chicken for 10 minutes on each side, or until the juice ares clear when tested with a toothpick. Let the meat stand for 5 minutes before shredding into thin strips.

Heat the extra oil in a small pot. When it is very hot, drop one or two prawn crackers into the oil. They will puff up in about 10 seconds. Take them out and drain on paper towel. Repeat until all the crackers are done.

Combine the carrot, onion, cabbage, chicken and herbs in a bowl. Five minutes before serving, toss the sauce through the salad, and sprinkle the fried shallots over.

Serve the salad with the prawn crackers, so guests can help themselves by having a bit of salad on a cracker as a bite.

Hint: Add the sauce to the salad just 5 minutes before serving.

Nguyet Tran, Clayton, VIC

Spicy stuffed Fish in Banana leaves

Serves 6

This is a barbecue special for any celebratory occasion, but especially when we have visitors from overseas — usually from the UK in January or February. It showcases Sydney fish and is a hit as it looks spectacular and tastes great.

Ingredients

1 onion, finely chopped

3 garlic cloves, chopped

1 small knob ginger, chopped

2 red chillies, finely chopped

vegetable oil, for frying

4 tablespoons curry powder

1 sprig curry leaves

½ cup (50 g) dry breadcrumbs

1 cup (150 g) crushed cashews or peanuts

2 cups (500 ml) coconut milk

salt and pepper

1 large (about 1.5 kg) white fleshed fish (such as bonito or king fish), gutted and cleaned

1 lemon grass stalk, bruised (save the outer leaves)

banana leaves, for cooking

fresh coriander, chopped red chillies, lemon or lime slices, to garnish

steamed rice, to serve

onion and tomato salsa, to serve

METHOD

Fry the onion, garlic, ginger and chilli in oil until soft, then add the curry powder, curry leaves, breadcrumbs and nuts and lightly fry until mixture just turns brown. Stir in 1 cup of the coconut milk, or just enough to moisten the mixture. Season to taste with salt and pepper. Reserve ½ cup of this mixture.

Stuff the cleaned fish with the remaining mixture and add the lemon grass and a few sprigs of coriander to the top of the stuffing. Wrap the fish in banana leaves that have been softened by pouring boiling water over them or by searing over a gas flame. Use the outer leaves of the lemon grass to tie the banana leaves.

Cook on a covered barbecue or over coals for 35–40 minutes. Meanwhile make a curry sauce using the remaining cup of coconut milk and the reserved nut mixture. Add extra curry powder and a teaspoon of turmeric if desired. Adjust seasoning and chilli to taste.

Unwrap the fish and garnish with the coriander, chillies and slices of lemon or lime.

Serve with steamed rice and an onion and tomato salsa.

Note: A simpler sauce using soy sauce and chopped chilli and coriander can be used if you like.

Kumar Pereira, Balmain, NSW

Spicy Summer Salad
Serves 4

I make salads all year round — summer, autumn, winter and spring. This spicy salad always goes down well on hot summer days and is a great accompaniment to an Australia Day barbecue. Alternatively, serve it warm with bread for a winter Sunday feast. It was borrowed and bastardised from a number of sources. People always exclaim 'I never thought of chilli in a salad' — but it is addictive!

Ingredients

400 g can or 1–2 cups of cooked lentils
1 red onion, chopped
2 large tomatoes, chopped (or a punnet of cherry tomatoes, halved)
1 garlic clove, crushed
1 red chilli, finely diced
1–2 pieces preserved lemon, finely diced
olive oil
Juice of ½–1 lemon, depending on juiciness
salt and pepper
1 cup flat-leaf parsley, roughly chopped
1 cup roughly chopped, mint or coriander

Method

Warm the lentils, drain and place in a bowl with the onion and tomato.

Combine the garlic, chilli, preserved lemon, olive oil and lemon juice, season to taste.

Pour over the lentil mixture while the lentils are still warm. Fold through the herbs when slightly cool, but not cold.

Serve cold in the summer or warm in the winter.

Suzanne Howard, by email

VEGEMITE SOUFFLÉ
Serves 8

My son doesn't like sweet things. No chocolate, no cakes, no fruit. Nothing sweet. So what to make that is special to act as a birthday treat? Vegemite Soufflé!

I also had the cheek to make it for our French host while staying in France. It was a great success. Even those who don't much like Vegemite love the slight tang this gives the classic cheese soufflé.

This recipe is shamelessly borrowed and adapted from St Stephanie's Bible, The Cook's Companion. I owe her my eternal gratitude for opening up a vast world of new flavours.

INGREDIENTS
4 tablespoons freshly grated parmesan cheese
30 g butter
2 tablespoons plain flour (or rice flour)
1 cup (250 ml) warm milk
1–2 teaspoons Vegemite
5–8 tablespoons freshly grated parmesan cheese, extra
4 egg yolks
5 egg whites
freshly ground black pepper

METHOD

Preheat the oven to 200°C. Butter eight 1/2 cup (125ml) soufflé dishes (or a 1 litre soufflé dish) then coat with grated parmesan cheese (more parmesan will be required for the 8 dishes).

Melt the butter in a heavy-based saucepan, and stir in the flour. Cook gently for 2 minutes.

Gradually add the warm milk, stirring constantly. Bring to the boil and simmer for 5 minutes. Stir in the Vegemite. Stir in the cheese, take off the heat and stir in the egg yolks. Pour into a large mixing bowl. Beat the egg whites in a separate bowl until firm peaks form. Add a little to the cheese mixture and fold in well. Fold the rest of the egg whites into the cheese mixture. It should keep a frothy consistency.

Spoon into the prepared dishes and cook for 20 minutes (or 25 for the large dish).

Serve immediately.

Note: Cheeses that may be used, either singly or in combination, are cheddar, gruyere, parmesan, or jarlesberg.

John Branton, by email

ZUCCHINI WITH LEMON, MINT AND PINE NUTS

Serves 4

Towards the end of January, we always have a glut of zucchini from the garden. This is a made-up recipe which is lovely served with roast lamb on Australia Day, but would be equally good on crusty bread or with pasta. The quantities are only estimates.

INGREDIENTS

2 tablespoons currants
finely grated rind and juice of 1 lemon
1 red onion, chopped
3 garlic cloves, crushed
5 anchovy fillets in oil (save the oil to cook with)
olive oil
3 tablespoons pine nuts
dried chilli
4 zucchini, sliced
salt and pepper
good handful mint
fresh ricotta

METHOD

Soak the currants in the lemon juice. Sauté the onion, garlic and anchovies in the anchovy oil and add a few tablespoons olive oil. After a few minutes add the pine nuts and dried chilli. Stir for a minute then add the zucchini, currants, juice and rind. Stir occasionally over medium heat until softened. Season, and stir through the mint.

Crumble the ricotta over to serve.

Emily Hill, Mt Rowan, VIC

VALENTINE'S DAY

ARMENIAN NUTMEG CAKE
Serves 8–10

This recipe is a rather sensual delight, and would be suitable for Valentine's Day. It was given to me about twenty years ago, by the German wife of a man who was building a cruising yacht designed by my partner. They lived in a lovely house on Lake Macquarie and we spent some very pleasant evenings with them, while Heidi cooked for us.

I particularly love this cake as it's so easy to prepare, almost impossible to spoil, and delicious to eat. The nutmeg offers an unusual taste, and the top half of the mixture is quite moist.

INGREDIENTS

1½ cups (225 g) wholemeal plain flour
1½ cups (300 g) brown sugar
125 g butter
1 egg, lightly beaten
1½ tsp baking powder
1 teaspoon ground nutmeg
½ cup (60 g) chopped walnuts or almonds
sour cream or yoghurt, to serve

METHOD

Preheat the oven to 180°C. Grease a 20–25 cm cake tin.

Mix the flour and sugar together, and rub in the butter. Put half the mixture into the prepared tin.

Mix the egg, baking powder and nutmeg into the other half of the mixture. Pour over the bottom layer.

Sprinkle the walnuts or almonds over the top. Bake for 30 minutes. Serve warm with sour cream or yoghurt.

Barbara Waters, Murwillumbah, NSW

CURRIED CHICKEN
VOL-AU-VENTS WITH CASHEWS
Serves 12

I got this recipe from an old school friend. It is usually served with rice but I have added my own spin by serving it in individual vol–au–vents. It is a delicious creamy curry and looks rather impressive for a special dinner.

INGREDIENTS
olive oil, for frying
1 kg chicken breast fillets, diced
1 onion, chopped
1 teaspoon curry powder
2 chicken stock cubes
2 tablespoons plain flour
1 cup (250 ml) coconut milk
½ cup (125 ml) water
100 g cashews
1 tablespoon olive oil
12 large vol–au–vent cases
steamed vegetables, to serve

METHOD
Heat a little oil in a large frying pan and brown the chicken in batches; set aside.

Fry the onion until soft and then add the curry powder, stock cubes, flour, coconut milk and water. Bring to the boil and return the chicken pieces to the pan. Reduce the heat and simmer for about 30 minutes. Add more water if it is too thick. Stir in the cashews.

Preheat the oven to 180°C. Spoon the mixture into vol–au–vent cases. Place in the oven for around 10 minutes to brown the vol–au–vents.

Serve with steamed vegetables.

Larissa Dever, Greenslopes, QLD

FETTUCCINE, SMOKED SALMON AND CAPERS
Serves 2

INGREDIENTS
200 g fettuccine
1 teaspoon olive oil
1 garlic clove, crushed
2 dessertspoons capers in vinegar, drained
100 g smoked salmon, roughly chopped
150 ml cream
freshly grated parmesan cheese

METHOD
Cook the pasta in a large pan of boiling salted water.

Heat the olive oil in a pan with the garlic. Add the capers, smoked salmon and cream. Heat until simmering.

Drain the pasta then fold it through the salmon mixture. Serve immediately with parmesan. YUM!

Paul Pitkethly, by email

FIONA'S FAULTLESS EGGS BENEDICT

Serves 4

INGREDIENTS

4 slices crusty Italian bread
60 ml extra virgin olive oil
4 eggs
8 slices prosciutto

Sauce
375 g unsalted butter
5 egg yolks
80 ml lemon juice

METHOD

To make the sauce, slowly melt the butter in a microwave, 20 seconds at a time. Pour the melted butter into a jug. Place the egg yolks and lemon juice into a food processor. Process until creamy. While the motor is still running, very slowly pour in the butter, one-quarter at a time until the mixture thickens.

Brush the bread with the olive oil and grill both sides. Poach the eggs, drain and set aside.

Place the prosciutto on top of the toast, then the warm egg. Drizzle the sauce on top of the eggs while still warm.

Sauce turns out thick and perfect every time.

Fiona Hodges, by email

GAIL'S PASTA SALAD
Serves 2

When my husband was diagnosed with diabetes I started experimenting with different recipes. Pete loves potatoes but they are a no-no for diabetics. Pasta is very good but he is not keen on it. However, he loves this tasty salad.

INGREDIENTS
250 g pasta (small coloured spirals are good), cooked
50 g baby spinach
20 g basil leaves, torn
100 g sundried tomatoes, chopped (reserve 1 tablespoon oil)
75 g kalamata olives, sliced in half lengthways
50 g pickled baby cucumbers (cornichons), chopped
50 g pine nuts, toasted
grated or shaved parmesan cheese, to serve
sea salt and freshly ground black pepper

METHOD
Toss all the ingredients in a large bowl and add the oil from the sundried tomatoes. Season well with pepper and a little salt. Serve with the parmesan cheese.

You could add chopped grilled prosciutto if you like.

Gail Chapman, by email

Luscious Plums with Cinnamon Honey Cream

This is so easy it doesn't really qualify as a 'recipe'. The deep red of the plums would be fitting for Valentine's Day, but these could be served on any occasion early in the year when plums are at their peak. They look after themselves and allow the cook to relax and enjoy the company rather than stressing about what is happening in the kitchen.

Ingredients

red fleshed plums (Mariposa or Satsuma), allow about 2 per person
brown sugar
ground cinnamon
finely grated orange rind
lightly whipped, cream
honey

Method

Preheat the oven to 180°C.

Put the whole plums into a lightly greased ovenproof dish that is just big enough to hold them in one layer.

Sprinkle a generous layer of brown sugar over the top to suit the degree of sweetness desired. Sprinkle over some cinnamon and grated orange rind.

Cover with foil and bake for about 30 minutes in a moderate oven or until tender. The brown sugar will combine with the plum juices to make a beautiful deep rich red syrup.

Serve the plums just warm, with the whipped cream that has been flavoured with a little honey and cinnamon — plus a scoop of ice cream, if desired. They are also lovely served cold with Greek yoghurt.

Margaret Quill, Hillwood, TAS

MARIA'S CANNELLONI
Serves 4–5

My husband took me out for Valentine's Day and we ordered cannelloni. They came out with these thin dried up logs which were very disappointing. I told my husband that in future I would cook cannelloni for us my way. So every Valentine's Day I cook these and we have a candlelit dinner. After I had my three children they couldn't wait for Valentine's Day. So we used to have a family Valentine's Day.

INGREDIENTS

Filling
1 onion, diced
1 garlic clove, crushed
olive oil, for frying
500 g beef mince
2 tablespoons tomato sauce
½ cup (125 ml) water
1 potato, diced
1 carrot, chopped
salt and pepper

Sauce
2 large onions, sliced
1 garlic clove, crushed
olive oil, for frying
400 g can whole tomatoes, crushed
small bunch basil
2 teaspoons sugar

Pancakes
1 cup (150 g) plain flour
pinch of salt
1 egg
1 cup (250 ml) milk
olive oil, for frying
freshly grated parmesan cheese

METHOD

Preheat the oven to 180°C.

To make the filling, fry the onion and garlic in a little olive oil until soft. Add the mince and brown. Add the tomato sauce, water, potato and carrot. When it boils, lower the heat to simmer and cook until thickened. Add salt and pepper to taste.

To make the sauce, fry the onion and garlic in a little oil, then add the remaining ingredients and simmer until the mixture thickens.

To make the pancakes, sift the flour and salt into a bowl. Make a well in the centre and add the egg. Mix with the wooden spoon, blending in a little flour from the side when it begins to thicken. Add the milk and stir until smooth. Heat a little oil in a frying pan. Pour in ⅔ cup (170 ml) batter. Tilt the pan to spread the batter. Cook on one side, then turn and cook on the other side. Continue until all the batter is used.

Preheat the oven to 180°C.

Divide the meat mixture between the pancakes and roll up. Arrange in a rectangular ovenproof dish. Spread the sauce on top and sprinkle with the grated parmesan cheese. Bake in a moderate oven for 15 minutes.

Maria Fichera, Victoria Estate, QLD

Revealing Duck
Serves 2

Something a bit different ....

Move to Tasmania and live in countryside.

Acquire nutty next-door neighbour who wishes to raise ducks in your chook yard.

Ensure neighbour does not feed ducks enough food.

When their time comes (sob), ensure neighbour offers you one of the ducks for all your trouble.

Invite the fantastic new man in your life (NOT the neighbour!!!) to Valentine's dinner then look on the internet for the best orange sauce you can find.

Spend hours simmering whole oranges and spend lots of money on expensive liqueur to add to sauce.

Cook duck according to recipe book.

When man comes, serve him the duck with the expensive orange sauce and watch his face closely. When it eventuates that there is little meat on the duck, and what there is is dry and stringy — if he does not give it away, and tells you how delicious everything is and keeps on pretending to eat, this is the man for you!

Let man off by telling him he does not have to eat this disgusting meal, throw duck in bin and go out to Fee and Me in Launceston instead (well, the next day as it is booked out for Valentines)! Enjoy remains of liqueur later.

(This is a true story that happened to me while living in Bracknell, Tasmania, where I had moved to study nursing in 2005.)

Marjorie Dixon, Wainiassa, ACT

Rhubarb Champagne
Makes 5 litres

I got this recipe many years ago from a radio program on the ABC. It is always delicious, has a light pink blush and a delightful taste. Only problem is you have to remember to make it a week in advance of the celebration. I usually make it for Christmas lunch and serve it so cold it is slushy with ice. Delightfully refreshing on a very warm day, but can be a nice celebration drink for any time.

Ingredients
    1 kg rhubarb, cut into small pieces
    750 g white sugar
    1 dessertspoon vinegar
    5 litres water
    3 lemons, thinly sliced

Method
Mix all the ingredients together in a very clean plastic bucket. Stir until mixed, cover and stir occasionally for the next 48 hours. Strain into sterilised bottles and securely cap! Screw tops work best. Leave for 4 days. Serve very cold, almost to the point of being icy.

Margie Ward, by email

Richest Hot Chocolate Ever
Serves 2

Ingredients
¼ cup (110 g) dark chocolate melts
1 cup (250 ml) water
1 cup (250 ml) full cream milk
maple syrup or hazelnut syrup to taste (optional)

Method
Divide the chocolate melts between two mugs. Bring the milk and water to the boil in a saucepan. Pour over the melts and stir until smooth. Add syrup to taste for extra sweetness and decadence.

You will need a teaspoon to scrape up the chocolaty mud from the bottom of the mug.

Anna De Paoli, Queanbeyan, NSW

SIMPLE BUG TAIL FETTUCCINE
Serves 6

Fresh flavours perfect for a summer night and you won't be in the kitchen for long. Enjoy!

INGREDIENTS

1 kg cooked Moreton bay bugs
1 bunch asparagus
⅓ cup (80 ml) good quality olive oil
fresh fettuccine, preferably homemade
1 large red chilli, finely chopped and deseeded
2 garlic cloves, finely chopped
1 cup roughly chopped, flat-leaf parsley
½ cup (125 ml) good quality white wine
sea salt and freshly ground black pepper
flat-leave parsley leaves, to garnish

METHOD

De-tail the bugs, slice the meat and set aside. Trim the asparagus and cut into pieces approximately 3 cm long. Place into a heatproof bowl and cover with boiling water. Stand for 2 minutes, then drain and refresh under cold water.

Heat half the oil in a frying pan while fettuccine is cooking. Add the chilli, garlic, half the parsley and a pinch of salt and pepper. Simmer for 2 minutes to release the flavours. Add the white wine and simmer for 1 more minute. Add the bug tails, asparagus and the remainder of the parsley and toss for another 2 minutes or until the bug tails have just heated through.

Add the fettuccine to the pan and toss all ingredients together until mixed well. Serve garnished with a few leaves of parsley. Pour on a small amount of olive oil to each plate. Season to taste.

Nick O'Brien, Mt Martha, VIC

STRAWBERRY AND DARK CHOCOLATE CHEESECAKE

Serves 8–10

After a season of the White Chocolate and Raspberry Cheesecake it was time for a change, so this one came about. No reason why any sort of chocolate and fruit combination wouldn't work. How about Fig with White and Dark Chocolate Swirl Cheesecake?

INGREDIENTS

180 g crushed chocolate ripple biscuits
80 g melted butter
500 g cream cheese, softened
¼ cup (55 g) caster sugar
⅔ cup (170 ml) cream
2 teaspoons gelatine, dissolved in ¼ cup cup boiling water
200 g dark chocolate, melted
150 g thinly sliced strawberries (save a few halved strawberries to decorate the top)

METHOD

Mix the biscuit crumbs and melted butter and press into a well greased and base lined 20 cm springform cake tin. (Be wary of adding all the melted butter at once as the biscuits themselves are quite 'fatty' and too much butter can create an oily texture to the base. The biscuits seem to vary a little in oil content from batch to batch.) Refrigerate.

Combine the cream cheese, sugar, cream and gelatine mixture in a food processor (or mix with electric beaters). When well mixed, add the melted dark chocolate. Mix well. Pour the mixture into the prepared tin. Arrange the slices of strawberry vertically through the mix, top with the halved strawberries.

Refrigerate for about 3 hours, until set.

John Branton, by email

WAYNE'S GLUTEN-FREE RHUBARB CAKE

Serves 8–10

My husband loves sweets,
And I like to treat,
On Tamborine Mountain, it is either rhubarb or beets.
So, rhubarb I poach and beetroots I bake,
His favourite by far is my poached rhubarb cake.
Old fashioned it seems,
With its red silky sheen,
Mum would be proud, she thinks rhubarb's a dream.
At sixty-four years,
It certainly appears,
Her efforts in the kitchen have finally premiered.

INGREDIENTS

Poached rhubarb
4 rhubarb stalks, trimmed and cut into 2 cm lengths
1½ cups water
1 vanilla bean, split lengthways
2 tablespoons brown sugar
icing sugar and whipped cream, to serve

Cake mix
200 g almond meal
½ cup (75 g) gluten-free self-raising flour
4 free-range eggs
200 g caster sugar
200 g unsalted butter, melted and cooled

METHOD

Preheat the oven to 180°C. Grease a shallow cake tin.

To poach the rhubarb, place the rhubarb in a saucepan and cover with the water. Scrape in the seeds of the vanilla bean and add the sugar. Cook gently until a thick stringy syrup remains, taking care not to burn.

To make the cake mix, combine the almond meal and flour in one bowl. In a separate bowl, beat the eggs and sugar until light and fluffy. Add the cooled butter.

Combine the wet ingredients slowly into the dry ingredients, adding the poached rhubarb at the end. Swirl the rhurbarb through but do not overmix. Gently pour the mixture into the prepared tin.

Bake for 55 minutes or until a skewer inserted in the centre of the cake comes out clean. Transfer to a wire rack to cool. Once cool, remove from the cake tin (slide a knife around the edges where caramelised rhubarb is sticky).

Dust lightly with the icing sugar and add a dollop of whipped cream to serve.

Felicity Mandile, Tamborine Mt, QLD

EASTER

Caldo Tlalpeño

Serves 6

Through my job I met an Australian woman who had lived in Mexico for 10 years then returned to Sydney with her Mexican partner. Until I had eaten at Vicky and Roberto's house I thought Mexican food was just sour cream and cheese. I'd never understood how fragrant and delicate it could be. Caldo Tlalpeno is Mexico's answer to tom yum: spicy, sour and heartwarming. It's now a staple comfort food in my home.

Ingredients

1 white onion, finely diced
2 garlic cloves, crushed
olive oil, for frying
1.6 litres rich vegetable or chicken stock
1 carrot, diced
2 corn (or flour) tortillas
1–2 chipotle chillies in adobo sauce, depending on your taste
400 g can four bean mix
juice of 2 limes
1 avocado, diced
2 tablespoons roughly chopped coriander

Method

Sauté the onion and garlic until transparent in a pot with a little oil. Add the stock and carrot, and cook for about 20 minutes, until the carrot is tender.

Meanwhile, slice the tortillas into thin strips. Fry in oil until crispy.

Add the chilli and beans to the pot and cook until warmed through. Divide the lime juice and avocado between serving bowls. Top with the soup then the coriander. Pass the tortilla croutons separately.

Note: traditional tlalpeno soup is made with chicken, poached in the broth. Chipotle chillies in adobo sauce are available from specialty shops.

Anna Fedeles, Newtown, NSW

CAPSICUM AND MUSHROOM SALAD

If the capsicum and mushroom salad is to be used at a sporting or other function, select capsicums in the team's colors!

Capsicums come in four different colours; black (or dark brown), yellow, green and red. Select ripe, firm, evenly coloured ones.

Core and deseed the capsicums, and cut into 2 cm squares.

Mushrooms should be large, firm, brown and flat. Avoid those that are limp, broken or sweaty. The stems are very flavoursome and should not be wasted.

By volume, select enough mushrooms to make up about a quarter of the salad. Remove the stems and put them in with the capsicum pieces.

Cut the mushrooms into 2 cm squares and put these in the bowl with the capsicum pieces.

Make a dressing of good vinegar and good olive oil of about one-third vinegar and two-thirds oil. Pour these into a jar and whisk or shake until all is thoroughly blended. You may wish to add some herbs or pepper to the dressing.

Pour a little of the dressing over the salad. Toss or stir the salad until the capsicums and the mushrooms are evenly mixed and there is a fine coating of dressing on everything. The dressing should not flood the salad.

Serve in a glass bowl as an accompaniment.

Fred Franklin, by email

CHICKEN, FIG AND LENTIL TAGINE

Serves 8

This recipe is ideal for entertaining and is so easy to make.

INGREDIENTS

1 tablespoon olive oil
8 chicken thighs
2 red onions, sliced
1 teaspoon ground coriander
1 teaspoon ground cumin
1 teaspoon hot paprika
3 cm piece ginger, peeled and grated
3 tablespoons tomato paste
600 ml chicken stock
200 g dried figs, halved
100 g green lentils
small handful fresh coriander, chopped

METHOD

Heat the oil in a large heavy-based saucepan over medium–low heat and brown the chicken until golden all over. Add the onion, turn down the heat and cook for 5 minutes. Add the spices, ginger and tomato paste and cook for 2 minutes. Add the stock, figs and lentils and simmer over very low heat for 25 minutes or until the lentils are tender. Remove from the heat and sprinkle with the coriander. Serve with warm crusty bread, and a salad of green spinach leaves and vine-ripened cherry tomatoes.

Candy Brumpton, Mitchell, QLD

CHOCOLATE BAKED CHEESECAKE
Serves 8–10

INGREDIENTS
    100 g teddy bear biscuits
    60 g butter
    625 g cream cheese, softened
    395 g can sweetened condensed milk
    3 eggs
    family block soft-centered chocolate (mint, caramel,
        Turkish delight, etc), chopped

METHOD
Preheat the oven to 180°C. Grease a 20 cm springform cake tin.

Crush the biscuits (no fun if not teddy shaped, cooking should always be fun!), add the melted butter and press into the prepared tin. Bake for 5 minutes, 10 minutes for a crunchier base. Put base aside to cool a little.

Turn the oven down to 160°C. In a big bowl, beat the cream cheese until smooth then blend in the condensed milk. Add the eggs one at a time, beating well until combined. Pour the mixture into the tin, distribute the chocolate through the mixture. Cook for 1 hour. It's ready when the cake edge is pulling away from tin.

Leave in the oven to cool to stop cracks appearing in the cheesecake top.

Sally Birchall, Edmonton, QLD

CHOCOLATE BROWNIES
Makes 16

This is a simple, quick chocolate brownie that can be dressed up or down. It works well anytime of the year, for a special occasion or for a quiet afternoon tea. It is delicious with good quality chocolate and butter or with cheaper supermarket brands. I have used it with the sour cream frosting or just with a dusting of icing sugar. When short of eggs I have successfully replaced one egg with a mashed banana for a different taste.

INGREDIENTS
125 g butter
185 g dark chocolate (or use milk or even white)
1 cup (230 g) caster sugar
2 teaspoons vanilla essence
2 eggs, lightly beaten
1 cup (150 g) plain flour, sifted
½ cup (60 g) chopped pecan nuts (optional)

Frosting
100 g dark chocolate
¼ cup (60 g) sour cream

METHOD
Preheat the oven to 180°C. Grease a 20 cm square cake tin and line with baking paper.

Melt the butter and chocolate and place into a large bowl. Stir in the sugar and vanilla, then the eggs, sifted flour and pecans. Pour the mixture into the prepared tin and bake for 30 minutes. Cool in the tin. Turn out and spread with the frosting (or just sift icing sugar over if you like). Refrigerate until the frosting sets before cutting. Store in the refrigerator.

To make the frosting, melt the chocolate then stir in the sour cream. Stir constantly until the mixture is smooth and glossy.

Sandra Gormley, by email

CHOCOLATE ÉCLAIRS
Makes about 15

This is a recipe that I have been making for about 30 years. Whenever I am asked to bring a plate I like to make these éclairs as people can pick them up in their hands and eat them without needing a spoon. They are very popular with the men, and I have even taken them to functions where there haven't been many left at suppertime as the container has been opened and quite a few have disappeared before getting out onto a plate!

INGREDIENTS
1 cup (250 ml) water
125 g butter
1 cup (150 g) plain flour
4 eggs
whipped cream or thick custard, to fill
melted chocolate and butter, to ice

METHOD
Preheat the oven to 200°C and grease a baking tray.

Put the water and butter into a saucepan and bring to a full, rolling boil. Add the flour, remove the saucepan from the stove and stir vigorously with a wooden spoon. The mixture should hold together in a soft mass and leave the sides of the saucepan when sufficiently mixed. Add the eggs, one at a time and beat thoroughly after each addition until glossy and smooth. Spoon into a piping bag, and pipe into 6 cm lengths onto the prepared tray. Bake for 30–40 minutes, before lowering the temperature to 140°C to dry out the pastry. Cool on a wire rack, then cut in half lengthways and scoop out any soft mixture inside. Fill with the cream or custard, and ice with the chocolate that has a teaspoon of butter melted into it. Place the éclairs in the fridge to set the icing.

Note: During the initial high temperature cooking, don't open the oven door as the shells may not rise properly.

Dawn Morey, Warragul, VIC

EASTER HALVA
Makes 16 pieces

Every Easter my Greek mother-in-law made Easter Halva, which is a delicious Greek cake with syrup poured over. This recipe has been passed to me and I am now doing it for the family at Easter.

INGREDIENTS
125 g butter
½ cup (115 g) caster sugar
3 eggs
2 cups (250 g) semolina
½ cup (75 g) plain flour
1 teaspoon baking powder
2 teaspoons ground cinnamon
1 teaspoon ground cloves
1 cup (155 g) chopped blanched almonds
¾ cup (185 ml) full cream milk

Syrup
2½ cups (575 g) caster sugar
2½ cups (625 ml) water
1 cinnamon stick
a few whole cloves

METHOD
Preheat the oven to 180°C and grease a 20 cm square cake tin.

Beat the butter and sugar together. Add the eggs one at a time. Sift the dry ingredients and add alternately with the milk into the butter mixture with the almonds. Pour the mixture into the prepared tin and bake for 40–45 minutes until golden brown.

Boil the syrup ingredients together for 5 minutes and pour over the halva. Cool and cut into squares.

Victoria Mavros, Sale, VIC

FIG SALAMI
Serves 10–12

Feasts are associated with an abundance of food, and figs are an abundant fruit.

INGREDIENTS

1½ cups (260 g) finely chopped dried figs
3–4 tablespoons port, sherry, maderia, brandy or Galliano or Midori
⅓ cup (60 g) finely chopped dried apricots, if desired
½ cup (90 g) chopped sultanas
½ cup (65 g) crushed pistachios
1 cup (100 g) almond meal
8–12 slivered almonds

METHOD

Cut a piece of plastic wrap, about 20–22 cm wide.

Place the figs into a wide shallow bowl — preferably a single layer to ensure the liquid soaks into all the fruit and aids the softening process. Pour the liquid of your choice over the figs.

Soak for 15 minutes, then add the apricots and sultanas. Mix the dried fruit until the mixtures adheres and is blended. Add the pistachios and almond meal. Mix in well. Lastly, add the slivered almonds. You may wish to spread out the mixture and place almonds in the middle.

Place the mixture onto the plastic wrap and roll up to form a compact log shape. Wrap the plastic around the fig mixture, leaving ends open if you like. Lightly pound the fig mixture to ensure the dried fruit is well blended. Twist or fold the ends to seal. Store in an airtight container, in a cool dark place for 3–4 weeks.

To serve, cut into thin slices. Serve with cheese and biscuits accompanied by your favourite drink.

Helen Cretan, Lavington, NSW

GINGER FLUFF SPONGE
Serves 6–8

This recipe is old — possibly as old as I am. Not sure where it came from, it could have been my mother's. It is a favourite wherever I go, eaten up quickly and frequently requested. I love it.

INGREDIENTS
4 eggs, separated
1 cup (230 g) caster sugar
⅓ cup (40 g) cornflour
2 tablespoons plain flour
2 teaspoons ground ginger
2 teaspoons ground cinnamon
2 teaspoons cocoa powder
2 teaspoons baking powder
2 teaspoons golden syrup, slightly warmed
300 ml cream, whipped

METHOD
Preheat the oven to 180°C and grease two 20 cm cake tins.

Whisk the egg whites until stiff peaks form. Gradually whisk in the sugar and beat until dissolved. Add the yolks all at once and stir just until evenly mixed.

Sift the dry ingredients four times. Gently fold through the egg mixture, then lightly mix in the golden syrup. Spoon into the prepared tins and bake for 15–20 minutes, until the sponge shrinks slightly from the sides of the tin and is cooked. Turn onto a wire rack to cool completely.

Spread the cream onto one of the cakes then sandwich the other one on top.

Margaret Kavanagh, Moonee Ponds, VIC

KOURABIEDES (ALMOND COOKIES)
Makes 30–40

The holy week leading up to Easter Sunday is full steam ahead for the Greek housekeepers. Homes are cleaned and Easter specialties are prepared. These specialties are given as gifts when visiting friends and family during the Easter period. The gifts include candies, cookies (shortbreads), plaited Easter bread (tsoureki) and dyed eggs.

INGREDIENTS
200 g whole almonds
450 g soft butter
200 g sugar
3 egg yolks
4 tablespoons brandy
seeds from 1 vanilla bean
6 cups (900 g) plain flour
2 teaspoons baking powder
4 tablespoons rose water
icing sugar

METHOD
Preheat the oven to 190°C. Lightly grease 2 baking trays.

Lay the almonds on a baking tray and roast in the oven for about 5 minutes, then cool and finely chop.

Cream the butter and sugar in a bowl, add the egg yolks, brandy and vanilla seeds in that order. Sift in the flour and baking powder, add the almonds and mix together well.

Sprinkle your work surface with flour and tip the mixture onto it, kneading into a smooth dough. Roll out until just under 1 cm thick. Using the rim of a glass cut out small semicircles and place onto the prepared baking trays. Bake for 20 minutes. Cool on a wire rack, sprinkle with the rose water and icing sugar.

Myrto Aretakis, Bulleen, VIC

LAMB KEBABS MINUS THE SKEWER
Serves 10–12

This is one of the recipes I put in my monthly report (as District Livestock Officer). I subscribe to the idiom that the way to people's hearts is through their stomachs. I have had comment that people skip to the recipes, but sometimes they do look at the other details!

INGREDIENTS
- 2 kg lean diced lamb
- 2 garlic cloves, crushed
- 2 teaspoons salt
- 1 teaspoon grated ginger
- 1 teaspoon freshly ground black pepper
- 1 teaspoon ground turmeric
- 1 teaspoon ground coriander
- 1 teaspoon ground cumin
- 1 teaspoon ground curry powder
- 1 teaspoon dried oregano
- 1 tablespoon soy sauce
- 1 tablespoon satay sauce
- 1 tablespoon oil
- dash of chilli sauce
- 1 tablespoon lemon juice

METHOD
Place the lamb into a large mixing bowl and add all of the ingredients. Toss to combine and marinate for at least 3 hours, or overnight.

Barbecue or fry the meat in small batches so as not to take the heat out of the cooking surface, this will prevent the meat from 'stewing'.

Serving suggestion: place the cooked kebabs in pita or lavash bread and serve with some tabbouleh.

Edward Joshua, Dubbo NSW
Chef: Shirley Cahill

LASAGNE

Serves 6–8

This recipe was given to me by a friend many years ago and the first time I cooked it for my husband and four daughters it was a hit. Everybody loved it, which was a miracle! As my daughters grew up and left home one by one and had their own families, whenever we get together it has become our traditional family favourite.

INGREDIENTS

Meat sauce
1 tablespoon oil
1 onion, finely chopped
1 garlic clove, crushed
500 g beef mince
2 x 425 g cans chopped tomatoes
150 g can tomato paste
1 teaspoon dried oregano
1 teaspoon dried basil
1 teaspoon dried rosemary
1 teaspoon salt
½ teaspoon sugar

Cheese Sauce
60 g butter
3 tablespoons plain flour
2½ cups (625ml) milk
125 g grated tasty cheese
60–90 g mozzarella, sliced
½ cup (50 g) grated parmesan cheese
½ cup (125 ml) cream

250 g pre cooked lasagne sheets (try the green lasagne for a change)

Method

To make the meat sauce, heat the oil and sauté the onion and garlic for a few minutes. Add the mince and cook until brown, mashing any lumps of meat with a wooden spoon. Add the tomatoes with their liquid, the tomato paste and the remaining ingredients.

To make the cheese sauce, melt the butter in a saucepan. Stir in the flour and cook for 1–2 minutes. Gradually add the milk and stir over low heat until boiling. Add the tasty cheese and stir till melted.

In an oblong dish place alternate layers of the meat mixture, lasagne sheets then the cheese sauce. Repeat the layers ending with cheese sauce. Lay the mozzarella on the top and bake in a moderate oven until mozzarella melts. Combine the parmesan and cream and pour over the top and bake for a further 5 minutes or until slightly brown.

Serve with a tossed salad.

Marie Ann Spicer, by email

LEMON, POPPY SEED AND COCONUT BISCUITS

Makes 60

9.20 a.m. Oh no, slept in! Frantic. Right. Shower, check calendar.

9.30 a.m. People coming at 11.00 am. Farm dusty dry and horrid, not like in films or magazines. Closest shop with cooking ingredients half an hour away! What's in the cupboard?

9.32 a.m. No biscuits, no cake. Hmmmm Weet bix, various white powdery substances, vanilla essence and those ball bearing things for decorating cakes.

9.45 a.m. Dear me. What to do? Not really up to scratch for morning tea. Where are the children???

10.00 a.m. Aha! Old tragic looking lemon, half a packet of coconut, some poppy seeds, and a need to occupy the children.

10.01 a.m. Right. Plan of attack. Dress 1 and 3 year olds. Do speed clean. Cook biscuits with children (brave tactic — will have to clean kitchen and children again). Get changed. Welcome friends. Brew tea, serve biscuits. Eat, chat, laugh, giggle.

12.00 p.m. Phew! Did it. Am super farmer's wife, brilliant cook in vein of Maggie Beer using intuition and ingredients at hand. Am domestic goddess like Nigella but in Drizabone! Am fabulous!

12.01 p.m. Tiger snake in breezeway. Watched it come in through a hole the builder has not finished off where extension joint new building and old part of house.

I am calm. I am domestic goddess. I know what to do. Collect teddies, children and phone. Sit on top of kitchen table with children. Close glass doors, roll up towels to put around all door bottom. Watch snake through glass while we all eat yummy biscuits. Try to locate husband via phone — needed to relocate snake. Thank goodness for biscuits and cups of tea! I am calm. I am domestic goddess. I know what to do. Keep everyone safe and feed them.

1.30 p.m. All's well, snake gone. Need to cook more biscuits — have eaten them all.

Ingredients

250 g butter
1 cup (220 g) sugar
2 eggs
2 cups (300 g) plain flour
2 teaspoons baking powder
2 teaspoons vanilla essence
3 cups (270 g) desiccated coconut
juice and finely grated rind of 1 lemon
1 cup (155 g) poppy seeds
silver balls (cachous)

Method

Preheat the oven to 180°C and grease 3 oven trays (or line with baking paper).

Cream the butter and sugar. Add the rest of the ingredients and mix. Roll into balls the size of a ping pong ball (about 3 cm), squash slightly. Top each with a silver ball. Bake for 8–12 minutes until firm and slightly browned.

Louise Loane, Fingal, TAS

MARINATED PRAWNS
Serves 8

My friend Thamoney made this marinade, basted a chicken with it and cooked it in the oven on a slow heat for 3 hours and it was lovely. I thought I'd try it with prawns and I've always used it with prawns ever since.

INGREDIENTS

Marinade
½ cup (125 ml) tomato sauce
¼ cup (60 ml) plum sauce
1 teaspoon sweet chilli sauce
1 teaspoon oyster sauce
¼ cup (60 ml) water
2 tablespoons vegetable oil
3 garlic cloves, crushed
½ teaspoon dark soy sauce
½ teaspoon mixed herbs
pinch of pepper

2 kg green prawns
2 tablespoons butter
2 tablespoons oil, extra

METHOD

Mix all the marinade ingredients in a bottle and shake well. Mix in the prawns and marinate overnight or for at least 3 hours.

Heat the butter and oil in a frying pan. Cook the prawns in batches, turning occasionally, until the prawns turn pink or are cooked. Remove from the pan. Repeat the process until all the prawns are cooked. Bring the marinade to the boil and cook for 2 minutes, then add the prawns to heat through.

Bridget Larsen, Gordon, ACT

Nan's Baked Caramel Pudding

Serves 6

This recipe was passed to me from my Nan, who brought it with her when she and my grandfather came to Australia from New Zealand in 1938. It had been her mother's, and is now being made by my daughter, the fifth generation to do so.

Ingredients

60 g butter
½ cup (110 g) sugar
1 egg
1¼ cup (185 g) self-raising flour
½ cup (95 g) mixed dried fruit or chopped raisins
⅓ cup (80 ml) milk
1 teaspoon vanilla essence
1 cup (250 ml) water
1 cup (200 g) brown sugar
60 g butter, extra

Method

Preheat the oven to 180°C.

Cream the butter and sugar, add the egg and alternately the flour, fruit, milk and vanilla. Put into a greased ovenproof dish. Combine the water, brown sugar and extra butter in a saucepan and bring to the boil. Pour over the cake mixture. Bake for 30–45 minutes.

Serve hot with ice cream or custard.

Linda Mill, Delungra, NSW

OCEAN TROUT AND DILL MAYONNAISE
Serves 4

INGREDIENTS
1 whole ocean trout, cleaned
2 lemons, sliced
1 bunch dill
2 glasses white wine

Mayonnaise
2 egg yolks
1 cup (250 ml) extra virgin olive oil
1 teaspoon Dijon mustard
sea salt and freshly ground black pepper
juice of 2 lemons
¼ cup (60 ml) cream, whipped

METHOD
Preheat the oven to 180°C.

Wipe the fish over, and cut through the back bone in 6 places with a sharp knife. Place a lemon slice or 2 in every cut.

Reserve 3 stalks of the dill, and stuff the fish with the remaining dill and lemon slices. Layer 3 sheets of foil on a baking tray and place the fish onto the oiled foil. Turn up the edges, pour over the white wine, and then make an envelope with 3 layers of foil on top. Cut some steam holes in the parcel.

Place in the oven and cook for 40 minutes. Take the tray from the oven carefully, and let cool slightly before opening the foil (be careful, as the steam is hot).

The fish is best served at room temperature, but in hot climates it can be covered and refrigerated for a few hours.

To serve, display the fish on a large platter, with quartered lemons and the mayonnaise.

To make the mayonnaise, place the egg yolks into a glass bowl. Dribble in the oil, whisking all the time, until the mixture has thickened and absorbed all the oil. Add the mustard, salt and pepper to taste and enough lemon juice to create a thick creamy sauce. Add the reserved dill, and just before serving, add the cream and mix thoroughly.

Dian Ball, Bowral, NSW

Steamed Fish with Lemon Myrtle and Capers

Serves 2

Good Friday calls for a purely delicious fish dish. Here I created, with the help of my then two-year-old daughter, something we all now share often throughout the year. I combined the flavours from the depth of the seas with those of leaves from the height of the trees.

Ingredients

- 2 tablespoons olive oil
- 1 tablespoon butter
- 1 bunch broccolini, trimmed and cut into 3
- 16 green beans, whole
- 1 small red capsicum, thinly sliced
- 10 cherry tomatoes, halved
- 2 purple garlic cloves, crushed
- 1 tablespoon salted capers, rinsed well
- 2 pieces firm flesh fish of your choice
- 4 lemon myrtle leaves
- juice of 2 lemons (or 1 lime)
- salt and pepper

METHOD

Heat a frying pan, add the olive oil and butter. Place the vegetables into the pan and stir fry over a moderate heat, until cooked. Add the garlic and half of the capers. Stir until the garlic becomes fragrant, then move the vegetables to the edge of the pan and reduce the heat to low.

Lay the fish in the centre of the pan, scatter with the remaining capers, and the lemon myrtle leaves.

Squeeze the lemon juice over the fish and immediately put the lid on (or foil if you don't have a lid).

Steam for 8–10 minutes or until the fish is cooked through. This will vary depending on the thickness of the fillet. If the fillets are thick, check that there is enough liquid in the pan so nothing sticks. Add more lemon juice if necessary. Remove the lid, stir vegetables and check whether the fish is cooked.

Season to taste.

When cooked, discard the lemon myrtle leaves and pile the vegetables onto two plates, placing the fish fillets on top. Drizzle with the remaining juices to serve. This can be served with steamed rice on the side if you wish.

Emma Elizabeth Pears, Burwood East, VIC

Steamed Golden Syrup and Ginger Sponge
Serves 6–8

Our favourite festive pudding given to me by a friend and neighbour from Central Queensland, many years ago. This recipe is truly magical ... and delicious too.

Ingredients
100 g butter
½ cup (115 g) caster sugar
3 eggs
1 cup (150 g) self-raising flour, sifted
½ teaspoon baking powder, sifted
½ teaspoon vanilla essence
¼ cup (60 ml) milk
½ cup (125 ml) golden syrup
¾ cup crystallised ginger

Method
Preheat the oven to 150°C.

In a mixer cream the butter and sugar until smooth. Beat in the eggs one at a time.

Add the flour and baking powder. Next add the vanilla and milk and mix well. Grease a small pudding mould and pour the golden syrup and ginger into the base.

Pour in the batter, place the mould in a shallow baking dish and fill dish three-quarters full with hot water. Cover with foil and bake for 1¼ hours.

Enjoy with ice cream or custard.

Bronwyn Laracy, by email

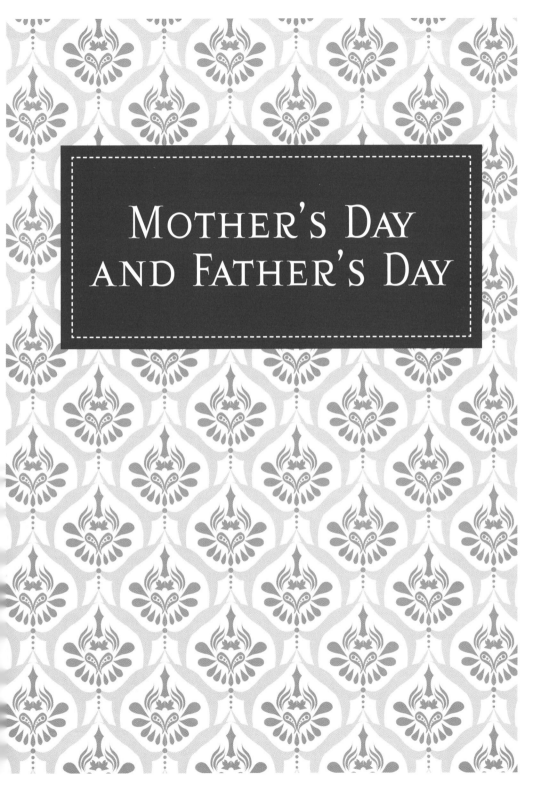

MOTHER'S DAY AND FATHER'S DAY

Apple and Blueberry Shortcake

Serves 6–8

This is an easy and delicious shortcake and the dough is very versatile. If you have leftover dough you can make great biscuits out of it, just make them to the shape you like and bake them at 180°C for 15–20 minutes and bingo. My dad grows a lemonade lemon tree and the lemons off it are the best, they are sweet but still nice and sour. They are perfect for this recipe (and in my opinion any recipe using lemons), the zest is best when it's green, just for aesthetics. I don' t know if anyone produces them commercially, but take my advice — buy a lemonade lemon tree and grow your own.

Ingredients

5 Granny Smith apples
2 tablespoons white sugar
finely grated zest of 1 lemon
1 tablespoon lemon juice
1 tablespoon water
125 g unsalted butter
125 g caster sugar
1 egg
1¼ cups (180 g) organic unbleached plain flour
1 teaspoon baking powder
1 cup (155 g) blueberries (frozen is great)
caster sugar, extra, for sprinkling
lemon zest, to garnish

METHOD

Peel and core 4 of the apples, and cut each one into about 15 pieces. Place the apple pieces, white sugar, lemon zest, juice and water into a small saucepan. Stew the apples over low heat for 10 minutes or until soft but not falling apart. Leave to cool slightly.

Cream the butter and caster sugar until smooth. Add the egg and mix until combined. Add the flour and baking powder and mix until the flour is incorporated.

On a lightly floured surface knead the dough, and when it has a smooth silky surface divide it into 2, wrap in plastic wrap and place in the fridge for about 30 minutes.

Peel and core the reserved apple and cut into cubes, add these and the blueberries to the stewed apples and mix gently to combine.

Preheat the oven to 180°C. Line the base of a 20 cm springform cake tin with baking paper.

On a floured surface, roll out one portion of the dough to fit the bottom of the cake tin. Place in the bottom of the tin and spoon the apple and blueberry mixture over of the base, making sure it's evenly distributed and that you leave a 1 cm border around the edge. With the second portion of dough, just using your hands this time, flatten it out to the same size as the base. Keep the lid rustic but don't let it fall apart. Place the lid over the base and press the two pieces of dough together around the edge. Gently brush with water and sprinkle with the extra caster sugar. Bake for 35–45 minutes.

Wait until it cools slightly before removing from the springform tin.

Serve cold with cream or just on its own with a cup of strong tea.

Daniel Young, Morwell, VIC

CHOCOLATE CARAMEL SLICE

Makes 16–20

My mum used to make this slice when we were kids. I still have the original recipe; carefully written out in my mum's handwriting on an old piece of notebook paper. I learned how to make the slice myself in my early twenties and now I have perfected it, Mum has been retired from the recipe. My dad especially loves it, and whenever we eat it we always end up reminiscing about the good old days.

INGREDIENTS

Base
1 cup (150 g) self-raising flour (substitute gluten-free self-raising flour, if required)
1 cup (200 g) brown sugar
1 cup (90 g) desiccated coconut
125 g melted butter

Filling
395 g can sweetened condensed milk
30 g (about a heaped tablespoon) butter, melted
2 tablespoons golden syrup

Topping
20 g melted copha
150 g dark chocolate melts, melted

METHOD

Preheat the oven to 180°C. Grease a slice tin and line with baking paper.

To make the base, combine the flour, brown sugar, coconut and butter in a large bowl. Mix well.

Press into the prepared tin, using the back of a metal spoon. Bake for 10 minutes or until lightly golden.

To make the filling, combine the condensed milk, butter and golden syrup in a saucepan.

Cook, stirring constantly with a wooden spoon, over medium heat until the mixture comes to the boil. Reduce the heat to low and stir constantly for 5 minutes. Spread the caramel over the base and bake for 10 minutes or until lightly golden. Set aside to cool for 1 hour.

To make the topping, combine the copha and chocolate melts, mix well. Spread over the caramel. Leave to set, then cut into squares to serve.

Nicole Kenny, Wynnum West, QLD

CHOCOLATE FRUIT AND NUT SLICE

Makes approximately 20

Catering an afternoon cocktail party for Mum, my sister and I had all the canapés and nibbles we needed but just wanted (yet) another something to serve with the coffee. I whipped this one up from memory, threw in a few new ideas — and barely a crumb was left. Experimentation since has lead to this one as the most popular version. Since my mum and aunt love this one so much — I'll dedicate it to Mother's Day. (I'm almost not allowed to turn up to any party without it now!) There's little cooking required, but as it needs to set in the fridge, best to make it the day before.

INGREDIENTS

   250 g natural sultanas
   60 ml orange liqueur
   60 ml hazelnut liqueur
   100 g diced mixed peel
   2 x 200–250 g blocks cooking chocolate (dark and/or milk)
   80 g unsalted butter
   1 tablespoon pure icing sugar (optional — just if you like it a bit sweeter)
   240 g slivered almonds, toasted and roughly chopped

METHOD

If you have time, put the sultanas into a small glass bowl, pour over the liqueurs and stir well. Cover the dish and leave them to soak anything from an hour to 3 days, if you like. Stir them occasionally.

Line a Swiss roll, lamington or similar baking tin with baking paper leaving the paper to overhang the sides (easier to get the slice out of the tin later).

Gently rinse the mixed peel then dry it on paper towel. (This is optional but it helps to remove the oil used in packing).

Melt the chocolate and butter together in the microwave or in a bowl over simmering water. (Make sure not to let any water or steam get to the chocolate.) When just melted, sift in the icing sugar (if using) and stir gently to combine. Set aside briefly, just to cool a little.

In a large bowl, combine the almonds, soaked sultanas (and any liqueur left in the bowl) and mixed peel. Stir until well combined. Add the still warm melted chocolate and butter mixture to the fruit and nuts. Working quickly, stir well to get a nice even mixture.

Pour or spoon the mixture into the prepared tin and spread it around to an even thickness. Smooth the top. (One of those silicon spatulas is great for this job; otherwise, just use a warmed metal tablespoon.)

Cover the slice with plastic wrap and chill in the fridge until set.

When ready to serve, carefully lift the slice out of the tin, holding the baking paper edges. Put the slice on a cutting board and with a large flat sharp non-serrated knife (if you have one), carefully cut into 2.5 cm squares. Try to cut straight down rather than saw through the slice.

Serve as is or dust with a little icing sugar — or top with edible gold leaf for a touch of glamour!

Note: Replace the liqueur with orange juice for a kids' version.

Elisabeth Thomas, Padstow, NSW

DAD'S HANDMADE BREAD
Makes 1 loaf

My children are always delighted when we stay with them, as they know I will make my special homemade bread, every day if necessary. As we live in Victoria, it is sometimes difficult to find a warm spot to raise the dough so the recipe and method have been modified so you can make a great loaf of bread any time, no matter how cold it is. What could be nicer for any special occasion than to serve up fresh, homemade crusty bread with olive oil and dukkah for nibbles, or just enjoy it as is.

INGREDIENTS
600 g quality bread flour
1 tablespoon bakers yeast (freeze dried)
2 teaspoons bread improver
1 teaspoon salt (or to taste)
2 teaspoons sugar (or to taste)
1 tablespoon extra virgin olive oil
500 ml warm water (350 ml cold water, 150 ml boiling water
    gives the ideal temperature of 38–40°C)
sesame seeds

METHOD
Generously grease a 1 kg bread tin.

Weigh out and thoroughly mix the dry ingredients in a large non–metal bowl, and heat in the microwave for 30–35 seconds on high. Also heat your cooking oven for 40–45 seconds to give you a warm spot to raise the dough (temperature should be 28–30°C after this).

Stir in the olive oil and gradually blend in the water until you have a moist but not too sticky dough (don' t worry if you don't use all the water). Mix the dough for a few minutes with a spoon but don' t knead it at this stage. Cover with plastic wrap and stand in the oven for 30–45 minutes, or until the dough has doubled in size.

Knock the dough out of the bowl onto a well floured board and dust the dough with flour. Cut the dough in half and knead each piece separately for about 5 minutes, adding flour as necessary if the dough becomes sticky. I find the simplest way is to stretch the dough by pushing it away from you, turning through 90 degrees each time, until the dough is elastic and not sticky. I finally form it into two balls and punch these down several times to expel any air.

Place the balls of dough into the bread tin, flattening each out as necessary so they fill the base of the tin, spray with water and add sesame seeds (or any other desired seeds). Return to the oven and leave for about an hour or until the dough is about 2 cm above the top of the tin. Turn the oven on at this point, about 175–180°C for a fan–forced oven, 200–205°C for a normal oven. Cook for 35 minutes, or until the bread sounds hollow when tapped underneath. When cooked, turn out on to a wire rack.

This bread will keep for several months in a freezer. I slice it the same day and seal it in a plastic bag for freezer storage. We remove slices as required, thawing them in the microwave for about 12–15 seconds per slice.

Tony Cavanagh, Ocean Grove, VIC

GHANA CHICKEN
Serves 4

In the 1960s my mother's cousin visited Ghana. In that era, transport connections did not easily allow Australians to travel to Ghana, consequently it seemed a truly exotic location to us. Perhaps the knowledge that the recipe came from a distant and unknown location added that extra little spice to an already delicious dish.

When my father died in 2005, my sister prepared a dinner for the family, choosing food that had happy associations for us all. Ghana chicken was the main course. It was a poignant occasion.

Every element of the following recipe has been altered according to the ingredients available. The essence of Ghana chicken is a rich tomato, peanut and chilli sauce.

INGREDIENTS
peanut oil, to fry
1 chicken
seasoned cornflour, to dust
2 tablespoons peanut butter
2 cups (500 ml) chicken stock
2 capsicums, chopped
500 g tomatoes
2 tablespoons soy sauce
3 garlic cloves
½ teaspoon cayenne pepper

METHOD
Heat the peanut oil in a pan. Dust the chicken pieces in the cornflour and fry in batches until golden. Set the chicken aside, and drain the excess oil from the pan.

Place the peanut butter into a bowl and add the stock gradually, stirring until smooth. Combine with the remaining ingredients in the pan to make a sauce. Return the chicken to the pan, and simmer until cooked through.

Penny Watsford, by email

MITETEI ('SKINLESS' ROMANIAN SAUSAGES)

Makes 10–12

This simple recipe is served traditionally in most Romanian households as part of any gathering or celebration. I learned how to make these wonderful tasty morsels when I visited my Dad's remote picturesque village of Bogata with my mum and sister in 2004. They are perfect for parties, barbecues or even cold for picnics.

INGREDIENTS

Sausages
1 kg pork and veal mince
pinch of both hot and sweet paprika
1 heaped teaspoon of bicarbonate soda
salt and pepper
crushed garlic cloves
2 onions, finely chopped and sautéed
1 egg, lightly beaten
1 large handful thyme and parsley, chopped
1 cup (250 ml) mineral water

plain flour, to dust
oil, for frying

METHOD

Mix all the sausage ingredients and leave overnight. Shape into sausage 'logs'. Roll in the flour and lightly fry in the oil until browned and cooked through.

They can be eaten hot or cold, smothered in tomato relish or a favourite mustard.

Sonia Muir, Orange, NSW

MUM'S MYSTERY CAKE
Serves 8–10

This was always the staple cake when we were young so it was always there when we returned home. On the occasions that I asked Mum for the recipe she always said, 'it's a bit of a mystery and it's not written down because it's different every time, depending on the ingredients available'. Here is the version I use, as I watched my mother make it on one occasion and wrote down the ingredients as it took shape.

INGREDIENTS

Base
1 cup (150 g) plain flour
2 tablespoons icing sugar
125 g butter

Filling
125 g walnuts, chopped
½ cup (60 g) sultanas

½ cup (45 g) desiccated coconut
¾ cup (165 g) sugar
1 teaspoon vanilla essence
¼ cup (30 g) plain flour, sifted
pinch of salt, sifted
1 teaspoon baking powder, sifted
2 eggs

METHOD

Preheat the oven to 180°C. Generously grease a baking tin.

To make the base, sift the flour and icing sugar together, and rub in the butter. Spread evenly into the prepared tin and press down lightly.

To make the filling, combine the walnuts, sultanas and coconut. Beat the eggs with the sugar and vanilla. Add the flour, salt and baking powder, then the fruit mixture. Blend well then spread over the base in the tin. Bake for 1 hour, until lightly golden and firm. Stand in the tin for a few minutes before turning out to cool.

Edna Russell, by email

MUM'S RUSSIAN BEETROOT SALAD
Serves 6–8

On arriving in Australia in 1949 as a displaced person from Europe, my Russian mother craved the food of her homeland but it was difficult to buy. I was embarrassed to be different from other children so I settled for Vegemite sandwiches in school lunches. However, Mum's beetroot salad was welcomed even though pickled herrings to accompany it were difficult to purchase. As a child I loved peeling the cooked beetroots and having pretty pink hands in the process. In those days, pickled herrings were not my favourite food but I really love them now! They bring back many childhood memories.

INGREDIENTS

2 carrots, unpeeled
2 beetroots, unpeeled
3–4 medium sized potatoes, unpeeled
1 tablespoon vinegar
½ teaspoon mustard
1 tablespoon oil
salt and pepper
1 onion, finely chopped
2 dill gherkins, cut into dice
1 cucumber, peeled and cut into dice

METHOD

Cook the carrots and beetroot until tender. Cook the potatoes separately. Allow to cool then cut into dice.

Mix the vinegar and mustard, add the oil and salt and pepper to taste. Add to the vegetables.

May be served with herrings (salted or pickled) and sauerkraut.

Tammy Yelland, by email

Red Lentil Balls

Serves 6–8

These red lentil balls are one of several feast dishes from my mum back home in Turkey. They originate from the eastern and south–eastern regions of Turkey. They are easy to make, and are delicious, especially when wrapped in lettuce leaves. Serve warm as a nice vegeterian dish; or cold, as a salad or side dish. Do not hesitate to adjust the amount of spices and herbs to your liking. The bulghur variety in this dish is the fine version (as opposed to the coarse one) — available at Middle Eastern shops. You may also try this dish with green lentils, but they take longer to cook, so will need more water.

Ingredients

2 cups (500 ml) water
1 cup (250 g) red lentils
½ cup (90 g) fine bulghur (cracked wheat)
1 large onion, finely chopped
1 garlic clove, crushed
½ cup (125 ml) olive oil
1 teaspoon tomato paste (optional)
1 teaspoon cumin (optional)
1 teaspoon salt
¼ teaspoon black pepper
½ cup chopped flat-leaf parsley
½ cup chopped green onions
1 teaspoon paprika

METHOD

Bring the water to the boil in a pot, and add the lentils. Cook over low heat until the water is absorbed, and the lentils are mushy. Remove from the heat, and stir the bulghur into the lentils. Let the mixture rest for 15 minutes to allow the bulghur to soften and expand.

In the meantime, fry the onion and garlic in olive oil until lightly browned. Add the tomato paste at the last minute, stir and remove from the heat.

Add the fried onion and garlic to the lentil mixture along with the spices and salt. Lightly knead until the ingredients are mixed. Taste, and adjust salt and spices. Add the parsley and green onions, and lightly knead. Shape the mixture into egg shaped balls. Sprinkle with paprika, and serve with lettuce leaves.

Evrim March, by email

Roast Pork with Apples and Prunes

Serves 5

My father is American and the first time I cooked a Thanksgiving dinner for him I made a dish I had learnt and perfected when working for an Italian diplomat in New York. The sweet fruit matches the saltiness of the pork so well and I couldn't help feeling a little proud as I watched my father carve the roast that I had made him.

Ingredients

3 green apples, peeled, cored and cubed
4 garlic cloves
250 g pitted prunes
1 kg pork loin roast, without crackling
olive oil
salt and pepper

Method

Preheat the oven to 180°C.

Peel the apples, core and chop into cubes. Crush 3 of the garlic cloves and mix with the apples and prunes.

Cut the remaining garlic clove in half and rub over the surface of the roast.

Oil a baking dish, add the pork and coat the surface in oil. Roast for 15 minutes. Add the apples and prunes to the baking dish. Return to the oven for another 30 minutes. Check the pork is cooked through by inserting a skewer. If the juices run clear the pork is done. Check the apples and prunes have softened.

Cover with foil and sit for 10 minutes. Serve slices of roast pork with apples, prunes and juices.

Anna Fedeles, Newtown, NSW

Shoo Fly Pie
Serves 8–10

My husband is from Canada and it is traditional where he comes from to make Shoo Fly Pie for Mother's Day, which I learnt early on. This recipe has been passed down through the generations, from his great-grandmother's time. It is very sweet but very delicious too.

Ingredients
1 pie shell (I use good quality frozen short pastry, blind baked)
1 cup (250 ml) golden syrup
¾ cup (185 ml) hot water
¾ teaspoon bicarbonate of soda
1 egg, beaten

Topping
1½ cups (225 g) plain flour
1 cup (200 g) brown sugar, tightly packed
60 g butter, softened

Method
Preheat the oven to 200°C.

Combine the golden syrup, hot water and baking soda. Stir well, mix in the beaten egg, then pour into the pie shell.

To make the topping, combine the flour and brown sugar, stir well. Rub in the butter until the mixture resembles breadcrumbs. Sprinkle on top of the filling in the pie shell. Bake for 15 minutes, then reduce the temperature to 180°C for 30 minutes or until brown and bubbly.

Leanne Bree, Langwarrin, VIC

SAUSAGE STEW

Serves 6

In the days when the shops were shut on the weekends, mum's pantry and fridge were lacking ingredients to cook up a Father's Day feast for the extended family. Improvising with what she had in the house, Sausage Stew was created that day. It's not the most attractive looking meal but it's hearty, made with love and guaranteed to have everyone from grandpa to toddlers coming back for seconds!!! Dad likes to refer to it as a real bloke's meal, and now we create it each and every Father's Day.

INGREDIENTS

8 thin sausages
1 onion, diced
1 large green capsicum, diced
4 bacon rashers, chopped
500 g small pasta shells
1 can baked beans, warmed

METHOD

Cook the sausages, cut into 3 cm bits, and set aside.

Sauté the onion and capsicum until soft, then add the bacon and cook until browned.

Meanwhile cook the pasta shells according to the packet directions. Drain and set aside.

Mix all the ingredients together. Stand back and watch the family make it disappear.

Catherine Roberts, Box Hill South, VIC

WALNUT CHEESECAKE
Serves 8–10

This was my mother's favourite cheesecake which I always used to make on Mother's Day. One can use Marie biscuit crumbs or digestive biscuit crumbs mixed with some cinnamon instead of the shortbread crumbs if liked. It is a very good cheesecake.

INGREDIENTS

Biscuit Crust
75 g butter or margarine
¼ cup (55 g) caster sugar
175 g shortbread biscuits, finely crushed

Filling
225 g cottage cheese
3 eggs, separated
¼ cup (60 ml) golden syrup
¼ cup (30 g) plain flour
150 ml whipping cream
¼ cup (50 g) caster sugar
75 g walnuts, chopped
walnut halves, to decorate
icing sugar, to dust

METHOD

Preheat the oven to 160°C.

Melt the butter or margarine and sugar over a gentle heat and stir in the biscuit crumbs. Press evenly over the bottom of a greased loose-bottomed (or springform) 18–20 cm round cake tin. Chill while doing the filling.

Soften the cottage cheese in a large mixing bowl. Beat in the egg yolks, golden syrup, flour and cream. Whisk the egg whites until stiff then whisk in the caster sugar. Fold lightly into the cheese mixture together with the chopped walnuts. Spoon the mixture into the prepared tin and arrange walnut halves on top. Bake for 1½ hours or until firm but still spongy to touch. Turn off the oven, open the door and leave the cheesecake to cool in the oven for an hour.

Chill in the tin in the refrigerator for 2 hours. Ease the sides of the tin carefully away from the cheesecake and lift the cheesecake out on the tin base. Dust the surface with icing sugar and place walnuts around if wished.

This cheesecake can be made the day before required and left in the refrigerator until needed.

Felicity Rooney, Sale, VIC

BIRTHDAYS AND ANNIVERSARIES

BANANA CAKE WITH CARAMEL ICING

Serves 8–10

You will need about 4 overripe bananas for this recipe. The cake can be made and iced 2 days ahead; keep in an airtight container.

INGREDIENTS

250 g butter, softened
1 cup (230 g) caster sugar
3 eggs
1 cup mashed banana
2 cups (300 g) self-raising flour, sifted

Caramel Icing
60 g butter
½ cup (100 g) brown sugar, firmly packed
2 tablespoons sour cream
1½ cups (185 g) icing sugar

METHOD

Preheat the oven to 180°C. Grease a 20 cm round cake tin, and line the base with baking paper.

Cream the butter and sugar in a small bowl with an electric mixer until light and fluffy. Beat in the eggs, one at a time, beating well after each addition. Transfer the mixture to a large bowl, stir in the banana then the flour; mix well.

Pour into the prepared tin, and bake for 45 minutes, or until a skewer comes out clean when inserted into the centre of the cake.

Stand in the tin for 5 minutes then turn out onto a wire rack to cool.

To make the icing, combine the ingredients and spread over the cake.

Olive Wescerne, North Mackay, QLD

BILL'S CASSATA
Serves 8

Bill, my husband, normally does not like desserts. However, this Italian ice cream is the exception. I make it only for his birthday, that way it keeps it up there with special celebration foods. The combination of flavours is just spectacular, the almond essence layer, bitter sweet chocolate layer and the colourful glacé fruit layer all combine into a heavenly indulgence. It is one of those recipes that can be done over a number of days in stages, a week or two in advance if so desired. Just follow the steps and even a beginner cook will turn out a masterpiece.

INGREDIENTS

First Layer
2 eggs, separated
½ cup (60 g) pure icing sugar, sifted
½ cup (125 ml) pure cream
few drops of almond essence — do a taste test

Second Layer
2 eggs, separated
80 g good dark chocolate, melted and cooled
2 tablespoons cocoa powder made into a paste
    with 1½ tablespoons water
½ cup (60 g) pure icing sugar
½ cup (125 ml) pure cream

Third layer
1 cup (250 ml) pure cream
1 teaspoon vanilla essence or
    ¼ teaspoon vanilla bean paste
1 egg white
4 tablespoons pure icing sugar, sifted
finely chopped glacé red and green cherries, apricots, pineapple and ginger
30 g flaked almonds, toasted

METHOD

Line a 20 cm round cake tin or 26 cm loaf tin with plastic wrap.

To make the first layer, beat the egg whites until firm peaks form then gradually beat in the icing sugar. Fold in the lightly beaten egg yolks. Beat the cream with the almond essence until soft peaks form. Gently fold the cream into the egg mixture in two batches until combined but still light and airy. Pour the prepared tin, or a loaf tin. Smooth the top over, cover with foil and freeze.

To make the second layer, whisk the egg yolks into the chocolate, then mix in the cocoa paste until smooth. Whip the cream until soft peaks form. Beat the egg whites until firm peaks form, gradually beating in the icing sugar. Gently fold the egg whites into the cream mixture in two batches. Lastly fold in the chocolate mixture. Pour over the almond layer, cover with foil and freeze.

To make the third layer, beat together the cream and vanilla until firm peaks form; beat the egg white until soft peaks form, gradually adding the icing sugar. Stir the egg white mixture into the cream mixture. Stir in the chopped fruit and toasted flaked almonds. Spread this mixture over the chocolate layer. Freeze.

Wendy Fisher, Bundaberg, QLD

Birthday Yoghurt Pavlova
Serves 10

This recipe came about because 4 of our grandchildren in one family greatly love both fruit and yoghurt. As the parents prefer the children to have healthier food if possible, I decided to try yoghurt instead of cream as the family did not particularly like cream in pavlova filling. Now the children request one of Nan's pavlovas for their birthdays. The birthday child eagerly chooses the fruit to be used and enjoys decorating the pavlova.

Ingredients
1 cup (230 g) caster sugar
1 teaspoon vinegar
1 teaspoon cornflour
4 egg whites (65–70 g eggs)
500 ml thick strawberry yoghurt
Seasonal soft fruit as desired such as berries, mangoes, bananas, pineapple, passionfruit or kiwi fruit
1 punnet strawberries, halved

Method
Preheat the oven to 200°C. Mark a 22 cm circle on a large piece of baking paper to fit a large oven tray, ensuring that the pen line is on the underside of the paper.

Place the caster sugar into a small bowl and stir in the vinegar and cornflour.

Place the egg whites in a large, dry mixing bowl and beat with electric beaters until fairly stiff peaks form. Gradually add the sugar mixture and beat for 8–10 minutes or until the sugar has dissolved and the mixture is very thick.

Heap the meringue mixture into the centre of the marked circle on the oven tray and shape into a 22 cm circle, using the pen line as a guide. Make sure the outer sides are higher than the centre of the pavlova.

Reduce the oven temperature to 125°C and bake the pavlova for about 1½ hours. If it seems crisp and starts to brown lower the cooking temperature slightly and reduce the cooking time a little. Leave to cool in the oven.

To serve, place the pavlova onto a serving plate and fill with the strawberry yoghurt. Pile the selected seasonal fruits onto the yoghurt and decorate with the strawberries. Place tall birthday cake candles on the pavlova and serve at once.

Note: To prevent wastage of the four egg yolks leftover from the pavlova, they can be used in cake recipes to replace 2 whole eggs.

Annette Margaret Mouat, Mandurang, VIC

Chicken, Chorizo and Pea Risotto
Serves 4

I visit my parents once a week and eat my mother's fabulous cooking. On her last birthday I invited them over and cooked this recipe which was originally a 'chuck together', but we all enjoyed it so much I typed up a recipe.

Ingredients

4 cups (1 litre) chicken stock

2 tablespoons oil

1 onion, chopped

2 garlic cloves, crushed

1 cup (220 g) arborio rice

1 chorizo sausage, sliced

300 g chicken breast fillet, sliced

¾ cup (115 g) frozen peas

3 tablespoons butter

3 tablespoons grated parmesan cheese

1 cup baby rocket leaves

Method

Heat the stock in a medium saucepan. Heat the oil over medium heat in a separate large saucepan. Cook the onion and garlic for 3 minutes until soft and translucent, taking care not to brown. Add the rice and stir so the oil coats the rice grains. Add the hot stock to the rice mixture 1 cup at a time. Stir continually until the stock is fully absorbed before adding another cup of stock. Continue until all the stock has been used, about 15–20 minutes.

Meanwhile, cook the chorizo in a frying pan for 2–3 minutes until golden. Add the chicken and cook for a further 5 minutes until golden brown and cooked through.

When the rice is cooked, add the chorizo, chicken and peas and mix well. Stir in the butter and parmesan. Serve topped with rocket leaves.

Brendan Biltoft, Mordialloc, VIC

CHOCOLATE WALNUT CAKE
Serves 6–8

This cake has been a traditional birthday cake in our family since the 1950s. It was my Aunt Cleo's masterpiece. More often than not she made this cake for family birthdays.

Either Mum or Aunt Cleo used to pipe fancy patterns with whipped cream and the inscription of 'Happy Birthday' and the relevant name would be on it.

I recall one time just a few short years ago, my sister made this cake for my birthday. She added sugared violets for my November birthday. It looked beautiful.

It is and always has been a favourite with all of us. From the time the aroma from the oven fills the house there is anticipation of this cake being cut. There are never any leftovers.

INGREDIENTS

Cake
120 g unsalted butter
1 cup (230 g) caster sugar
2 eggs
2 cups (300 g) self-raising flour, sifted
pinch of ground cinnamon
½ cup (125 ml) milk
500 g finely ground walnuts

Syrup
1¼ cups (310 ml) water
3 teaspoons sugar
pinch of ground cinnamon

Chocolate Icing
500 g dark chocolate buttons
drop of milk

Method

Preheat the oven to 180°C. Grease two 18 cm springform cake tins and line with baking paper.

Cream the butter and sugar, then beat in the eggs. Mix in the flour and cinnamon alternately with the milk. Add the walnuts and mix well.

Divide the mixture evenly between the prepared tins and bake for 45 minutes.

To make the syrup, bring the water to the boil with the sugar and cinnamon, and reduce a little until the sugar is completely dissolved. Pour the cooled syrup over each cake. This adds extra moisture to the cake.

To make the icing, melt the chocolate in the top of a double saucepan, adding a small amount of milk when the chocolate starts to melt. Stir gently until the chocolate is smooth and shiny.

When the cakes are cool, sandwich the two cakes with a little of the chocolate icing. Completely cover the cake with the remainder of the icing.

This cake is delicious served with espresso or Greek coffee.

Desi Gaffiero, Toorak, VIC

CROQUEMBOUCHE
Serves 50

This recipe makes approximately 100 cream puffs, enough for 2 per person for a function for 50.

I have made three of these, each one to take the place of a traditional cake. The first one was for an engagement party, the second one for my mother's 80th birthday party and the third one for my husband's 60th birthday party. I purchased a special croquembouche cone, but you can make a cone from cardboard. It should measure 23 cm at its base and be 35 cm high. Cover it with foil.

INGREDIENTS

Choux Puffs (Make this quantity 3 times)
1 cup (250 ml) water
75 g butter, chopped
1 cup (150 g) plain flour
4 eggs

Cream Filling
4 cups (1 litre) thickened cream
¾ cup (90 g) icing sugar, sifted
3 tablespoons Grand Marnier or Cointreau

Caramel (make 2 batches)
1 cup (250 ml) water
2 cups (440 g) sugar

METHOD

Preheat the oven to 230°C and lightly grease 2 oven trays.

To make the choux puffs, combine the water and butter in a saucepan and slowly bring to the boil, stirring until the butter melts. Sift the flour onto paper, and when the mixture is rapidly boiling, pour in the flour all at once. Beat with a wooden spoon until a smooth ball forms and the mixture no longer clings to the side of the pan. Remove from the heat and cool slightly by standing the pan in a sink of cold water.

Beat the eggs in a bowl with a fork. Gradually add to the mixture a little at a time, beating well after each addition, preferably using a hand-held blender, until the mixture is smooth and glossy. Drop slightly rounded teaspoons of the mixture onto the trays, about 3 cm apart. Bake for 10 minutes then reduce the heat to 180°C and bake for a further 15–20 minutes. The oven door must not be opened for the first 25 minutes. The puffs should be firm to touch, crisp, golden brown in colour and light in weight when cooked. Remove from the oven, make slits in the sides of the puffs to allow steam to escape and return to the oven for a few minutes to dry out.

Repeat this process twice more, spooning half teaspoon quantities onto 1 tray with the final batch.

To make the filling, whip the cream and icing sugar until stiff peaks form. Fold in the Grand Marnier or Cointreau. Place into a piping bag fitted with a plain nozzle. Pipe a little cream into each puff.

To make the first batch of caramel, put the sugar and water into a frying pan and stir until the sugar dissolves. Bring to the boil and boil rapidly without stirring until the mixture starts to turn golden brown.

Place a croquembouche cone onto a cake stand or cake plate. Dip the bottom of each puff into the caramel and arrange around the cone, working from the bottom up, using the largest puffs first. If the caramel sets before you finish assembling, add a little water and stir over the heat until it liquefies.

Using homemade or commercial crystallised violets, dip the backs in caramel and use to decorate the croquembouche. Make another batch of caramel, cool then drizzle with two forks over the croquembouche.

Provide small tongs to enable guests to help themselves.

Note: To make crystallised violets, brush each flower with egg white on both sides and sprinkle with caster sugar. Place on a wine rack in a warm place to dry. This can be done in advance.

The puffs can be made in advance and kept (unfilled) in an airtight container in the fridge. Reheat the puffs in the oven for 5 minutes to dry out before using. Allow 3–4 hours to assemble the croquembouche if doing it on your own.

Judith Lynn Bell, by email

CUCUMBER AND
WATERMELON SALAD

This is a recipe I made up due to the over abundance of cucumbers and watermelons grown in my vegie garden this year. I first made it when I had rellies over for a barbecue earlier this summer, and it has now been copied and made for Aunty Glenni's housewarming, and Great Nanna's 90th birthday lunch!

INGREDIENTS
Equal quantities of cucumber and watermelon, cut into 1.5 cm cubes
(to fill whatever size salad bowl you wish to serve the salad in)
½ red onion, finely chopped
leaves from 2–3 sprigs of mint, finely chopped
splash or 2 of balsamic vinegar
freshly ground black pepper

METHOD
Gently toss the cucumber, watermelon, onion and mint in salad bowl. Splash over a little balsamic vinegar, and grind the pepper over to taste. Gently toss again.

Bronwyn Modra, Talgarno, VIC

Four Layer Chocolate Tart

Serves 10–12

My friend is a big fan of chocolate and is sometimes heard complaining that desserts are not rich enough for her. I created this tart for her 18th birthday, knowing that I had packed in chocolate in every conceivable way. She loved it, and has requested it as her present in the years since that birthday. She is the ultimate chocoholic though, so beware, this tart may not be for everyone.

Ingredients

Pastry
250 g butter
1 cup (125 g) icing sugar
pinch of salt
4 cups (600 g) plain flour
4 egg yolks
4 tablespoons milk

Cooked Layer
150 g butter
160 g dark chocolate
6 tablespoons cocoa powder
4 eggs
1 cup (220 g) sugar
3 tablespoons golden syrup
3 tablespoons sour cream

Fudge Layer
200 ml cream
150 g dark chocolate
1 egg yolk
2 tablespoons brandy
20 g butter, melted

Mousse Layer
110 g dark chocolate
30 g butter
⅔ cup (170 ml) cream
1 egg
1 tablespoon honey

Top Layer
100 g milk chocolate
250 g dark chocolate (70 per cent cocoa)

METHOD

To make the pastry, cream the butter, sugar and salt either in a food processor or bowl, then blend or rub in the flour. Add the egg yolks and stir or blend until the mixture looks like lumpy breadcrumbs. Add the milk. Blend or stir to incorporate the milk, then turn out onto your kitchen counter and pat it into a ball. Don't knead it or touch it too much or it will shrink in the oven. Squeeze it into a ball, then wrap in plastic wrap and refrigerate for 1 hour.

Slice the pastry into pieces about 5 mm thick, and use to line the base and sides of a 21 cm loose-based 6 cm deep tart tin. Push the slices together to get a smooth crust, and tidy it up a bit by adding extra pastry to parts that look a bit thin and uneven. Freeze for 1 hour. Preheat the oven to 180°C. Bake the pastry for 15 minutes.

For the cooked layer, reduce the oven to 150°C. Put the butter, chocolate and cocoa in a saucepan and stir over low heat until smooth. Cream the eggs and sugar in a bowl and add the golden syrup and sour cream. Stir in the chocolate mixture and mix well. Pour into the tart shell, bake for 40 minutes and allow to cool.

For the fudge layer, heat the cream until nearly boiling, remove from the heat and add the chocolate. Stir until the chocolate melts, then add the egg yolk and brandy. Allow to cool a bit then stir in the butter. Pour this over the cooked layer of the tart and refrigerate for 1½ hours before proceeding.

To make the mousse layer, melt the chocolate and butter over low heat and cool. Whip the cream until stiff peaks form. In a separate bowl, combine the egg and honey then fold in the chocolate mixture and cream. Make sure you do this gently so that the air isn't lost from the cream. Pour over the fudge layer and refrigerate for an hour.

To make the top layer, grate the milk chocolate, and sprinkle over the mousse layer of the tart. With a vegetable peeler, shave the dark chocolate over the milk chocolate. Cut the tart into slices and serve with plenty of cream and seasonal fruit.

Kate Redman, Buderim, QLD

GOLDEN SYRUP DUMPLINGS
Serves 4

When my husband first began visiting me at home, my mother made him Golden Syrup Dumplings because his gran used to cook them. Unfortunately they were sodden and tough. She had lifted the lid to see how they were cooking — fatal mistake. I now routinely make them for him on his birthday, nearly always fluffy. One of the few things I can turn out better than my mother.

INGREDIENTS
1 cup (150 g) self-raising flour
pinch of salt
1 egg, lightly beaten
milk, as needed
1 tablespoon melted butter
½ cup (110 g) sugar
½ cup (125 ml) golden syrup
2 cups (500 ml) water
custard or ice cream, to serve

METHOD
Sift the flour and salt into a bowl. Add the egg and enough milk to make a stiff dough. Add the melted butter.

Combine the sugar, golden syrup and 2 in a large saucepan with a fitted lid. Bring to the boil. Roll the dough into balls the size of a ping pong ball and drop into the boiling syrup mixture. Simmer for 15 minutes. Serve with custard or ice cream.

Ruth Turpin, Echuca, VIC

GRANDMA'S CHOCOLATE CROWNS
Makes 24

Patty cakes, Anzac biscuits, melting moments, cream sponge and chocolate cakes are nostalgic of tea time in the '30s. These treats come still from my kitchen for the pleasure of my family on birthdays, Cup day, Sunday afternoons and also for lunch boxes.

During the 1930s in jobless depression years, my resourceful mother passed word around that she would bake to order. Pies, pastries, jam rolls and jelly cakes, Christmas cakes, plain or decorated, even a tiered wedding cake and biscuits. Requests poured in, many becoming regular orders.

Chocolate crowns were in frequent demand for Golf Club suppers, card parties and twenty-first birthday teas. They are dainty chocolate domes baked in gem irons, inverted and coated with chocolate icing. Serve split and filled with whipped cream.

INGREDIENTS
125 g butter
1 cup (230 g) caster sugar
1 teaspoon vanilla essence
2 eggs
2 cups (300 g) self-raising flour
1 heaped tablespoon cocoa powder
¼ cup (60 ml) milk
chocolate icing and whipped cream, to serve

METHOD
Preheat the oven to 180°C.

Cream the butter and sugar with vanilla. Add the eggs one at a time, beating well between each. Sift the flour and cocoa together, and stir in alternately with the milk. Grease and heat 2 gem iron trays. Drop 1 tablespoon mixture into each gem iron. Bake for 15 minutes. Invert onto a wire rack to cool.

Ice with chocolate icing, and fill with whipped cream.

Sybil Spall, Ivanhoe, VIC

LOWIE'S BIRTHDAY PAVS
Serves 8

This recipe is important to me because of its significance in my family with regard to birthdays. We as a family had neighbours who still hold a special place in our hearts. Mr and Mrs Lowe were known to us as Lowie and Mr Lowie. Every birthday Lowie had a pavlova ready for us and a present. One birthday in particular stands out, my dad's 50th. He had grumbled the year before that he would like more than just one piece of pav. Lowie, a fabulous listener, remembered this complaint, and when the pav came out after dinner there were two. One was sat down in front of Dad, the other in front of Mum to cut for us all. Lowie has since passed away but the tradition of pav for milestone birthdays still remains with us. By the way my dad ate the whole pav, and was crook the next day.

INGREDIENTS

Pavlova
2 egg whites
1½ cups caster sugar
2 teaspoons cornflour
1 teaspoon vinegar
1 teaspoon vanilla essence
⅓ cup (80 ml) boiling water

Topping
whipped cream
strawberries
kiwi fruit
banana
passionfruit

METHOD

Preheat the oven to 180°C and line a baking tray with baking paper.

Place all the pavlova ingredients into a small bowl and mix on high speed for 15 minutes. Spread onto the prepared tray. Bake for 10 minutes then reduce the heat to 120°C for a further 20 minutes.

When cool decorate with the cream and fruit. This may be changed with what is in season.

Andrea Nunn, Top Camp, QLD

MAARTJE'S APPLECAKE
Serves 6–8

Maartje is a good friend of mine in Holland, where we celebrated our birthdays with some neighbours and friends, having a cup of coffee at 10 in the morning. This was one of her cakes. Sometimes she spread apricot jam over the top.

INGREDIENTS
150 g butter
170 g sugar
finely grated lemon rind
pinch of ground cinnamon
200 g self-raising flour
3 cups (750 ml) milk
4 eating apples
lemon juice

METHOD
Preheat the oven to 160°C.

Mix all the ingredients (except apples) to a smooth dough. Put the mixture in a greased cake tin.

Cut the apples into quarters, and make cuts into the top of the apples. Brush with a little lemon juice to prevent them from getting brown. Arrange over the dough and push in slightly.

Bake for 1 hour.

Trijni van Dijke, Penguin, TAS

MANDARIN CAKE
Serves 6–8

This is a great cake for those who do not eat dairy or wheat. I can't remember where I got it — maybe from television or a friend. It works really well, is very moist and delicious and lasts for days (if not eaten immediately!).

INGREDIENTS
4–5 medium mandarins
250 g almond meal
1 cup (230 g) caster sugar
2 tablespoons baking powder

METHOD
Steam or boil the mandarins for 2 hours (doesn't matter if they are seedless or not as the seeds soften.)

Preheat the oven to 190°C. Grease and line a 22 cm springform cake tin, or ring pan.

Cool and blend the mandarins.

Combine with the dry ingredients and pour into the prepared tin. Bake for 1 hour or until a skewer comes out clean. Cool in the tin on a wire rack.

Depending on the dietary needs of consumers, icing sugar sprinkled over the top will do, with a flower from the garden, or mash a mango into ewe's milk yoghurt, or cream cheese if you can tolerate dairy products.

If they are in season and cheap, the mandarins can be steamed in batches and frozen — then they can be defrosted when you feel like making the cake at another time — this makes it very quick.

WARNING: Don't put the baking powder into the hot mandarin mixture in the blender. I did the first time I made this cake three years ago. I think it took most of the summer to find all the bits of mandarin in very unusual places in the kitchen from when it exploded.

Anne-Lisette Girard, by email

MUM'S CHICKEN POT ROAST

Serves 6

This is a wonderful way to cook chicken. As a child, whenever my mum asked me what I would like her to cook for my birthday, I would always answer 'your chicken pot roast'. As an adult, I realise that this is a very healthy way to cook chicken as it contains garlic, ginger and turmeric — three ingredients which are claimed to be excellent for our health. So not only is it very tasty, it is good for you too!

INGREDIENTS

1 whole chicken (preferably free range), chopped into pieces
½ cup (125 ml) white vinegar
light olive oil or sunflower oil
2 garlic cloves, crushed
3 cm piece ginger, finely chopped

1 teaspoon turmeric
2–3 cinnamon sticks
6–8 whole cloves
1–2 green chillies, optional, chopped
salt

METHOD

Remove the skin from the chicken and place in the vinegar to soak. Heat the oil in a large pan, and sauté the garlic and ginger for a couple of minutes. Add the spices and cook for 1 minute, stirring.

Remove the chicken from the vinegar and add to the pan, with the chillies, if using. Turn the chicken occasionally to brown. Lower the heat and cover the pan. The chicken will produce juices which cook the meat without adding any additional liquid. After 5–10 minutes, season with salt and stir well. Reduce the heat to very low and cook, covered, for 45–50 minutes. Check regularly to move the pieces and prevent catching on the bottom. The result is succulent yellow chicken pieces with very little liquid left in the pan. Excellent served with steamed basmati rice.

Susana Smith, by email

NANNA HOURIGAN'S
NO FAIL SPONGE
Serves 8

This is my mum's recipe. She had 11 children, and was widowed when 8 of them were still quite young. There was never much luxury growing up in our house, but you would always know that Mum would make the effort to make you this beautiful sponge for your birthday. I now continue that tradition with my own children, and have taught my two teenage boys how to make it.

INGREDIENTS

1 cup (125 g) cornflour
1 teaspoon cream of tartar
1 teaspoon bicarbonate of soda
1 cup (125 g) custard powder

4 eggs, at room temperature, separated
1 cup (230 g) caster sugar
whipped cream, to fill

METHOD

Preheat the oven to 200°C and lightly grease two 20 cm sandwich tins. Sift the dry ingredients (except the sugar) together at least 3 times. This guarantees a light fluffy sponge.

Beat the egg whites until soft peaks form. Add the sugar a little at a time, beating constantly. Add the egg yolks and beat just to combine. Sift in the dry ingredients, and fold in with a metal spoon. Divide the batter between the tins, and bake for 15–20 minutes, until the cake springs back when gently touched in the centre. With practice you will be able to smell when the cake is ready, rather than opening up and touching in the middle. Cool on a tea towel, and use fresh beaten cream as a filling.

Note: You can use cocoa powder instead of the custard powder to make a chocolate sponge if you wish.

Kerry Leanne Riella, Stratford, QLD

PERFECT PESTO PASTA

Serves 4

This great pasta can be served as an entrée or main course and it can be served hot (my preference) or cold as a salad. It is a dish that I made up one night because my husband had been working very hard and I wanted to give him a treat! It is now a firm favourite, and perfect for a lovely weekend birthday celebration lunch. It is also something that those of us who aren't 'Super Chefs' can make quickly and easily.

INGREDIENTS

1 packet pasta (dried or fresh)
1–2 tablespoons olive oil
4 chicken thigh fillets, cut into 2 cm dice
4 bacon rashers (or 8 slices prosciutto), chopped
100 g semidried tomatoes
1 jar of good quality pesto
100 g feta cheese, roughly chopped
2 tablespoons cream or yoghurt, optional (the recipe works well
    without it, but I find that the cream finishes the dish off nicely)
freshly grated parmesan cheese, optional

Method

Cook the pasta in a large pan of boiling salted water until al dente.

Meanwhile, heat the oil in a frying pan and cook the chicken and bacon over high heat until brown. Reduce the heat to medium and add the semidried tomatoes, heat through for 3 minutes.

Reduce the heat to low and stir through the pesto. Add the feta cheese and allow to melt.

Stir in the cream or yoghurt and warm through.

Drain the pasta, reserving a small amount of the cooking water. Add the pasta to the chicken sauce and mix well, adding the reserved water if desired. Sprinkle with the parmesan cheese if using.

Serve with a green salad, crusty bread and a glass of sauvignon blanc!

Note: If using dried pasta which takes 10–12 minutes to cook, put the pasta on to cook just as you put the chicken on to brown. If using fresh pasta, then put the pasta on just prior to adding the feta cheese and cream.

Felicity Prideaux, by email

Sour Cream Rhubarb Bars
Makes 20 bars

This recipe was given to me by an American friend, Jackie, when we were posted in Moscow in 1980 — we both loved rhubarb and could occasionally find it in the market. I make it whenever I have rhubarb but I have two friends who always ask for this instead of a birthday cake.

Ingredients
1 cup (220 g) white sugar
1 cup (125 g) chopped walnuts
1 teaspoon ground cinnamon
125 g butter
1 cup (200 g) brown sugar, firmly packed
1 egg
1 teaspoon bicarbonate of soda
1 cup (250 g) sour cream
1 teaspoon salt
2 cups (300 g) plain flour
1 cup (125 g) chopped rhubarb (1.5 cm pieces)

Method
Preheat oven to 180°C. Grease and flour a 22 x 33 cm cake tin.

To make the topping, mix the white sugar, walnuts, and cinnamon together and set aside.

In a separate bowl, cream together the butter and brown sugar until light and fluffy. Beat in the egg. Dissolve the bicarbonate of soda in the sour cream. Add to the butter mixture with the salt, and then beat in the flour. Fold in the rhubarb. Pour into the prepared tin and sprinkle with the reserved topping. Bake for 45–50 minutes.

Ailsa Turrell, Kambah, ACT

SPANISH TART
Serves 6–8

The recipe was my mother's and I have never known anyone else to have it. It was our birthday treat, but my son, who had been overseas for many years, demanded this for last Christmas — above plum pudding and Christmas cake because Christmas came before his birthday!!

INGREDIENTS
¾ cup (115 g) plain flour, sifted
25 g butter

Filling
1 tablespoon butter
½ cup (110 g) sugar
1 egg, lightly beaten
juice and rind of 1 lemon
2 large apples, grated

METHOD
Preheat the oven to 180°C.

Rub the butter into the flour until mixture resembles breadcrumbs. Add enough water to bind together and knead lightly into a ball. Roll out and line a tart tin with the pastry.

To make the filling, cream the butter and sugar. Add the egg, lemon rind, juice and apples. Mix together. Place the mixture onto the pastry case. Bake in the oven for 20 minutes. Serve with cream or ice cream.

Margaret Weatherley, Albany, WA

STRAWBERRY HAZELNUT GATEAU

Serves 8–10

This has been my eldest daughter Alexia's birthday cake for nearly 30 years. Birthdays are really special in our family. The recipe has been adapted over the years from the original recipe from the Women's Weekly *cookbook. The recipe from 30 years ago was covered with cream, and the chocolate was just melted and was a bit hard. The cake was special as it heralded the start of summer and the strawberry season in those days (you can get fresh strawberries all year round now) as well as my daughter's birthday. It was usually hot as it was early November. It was very special in those days. The cake recipe is now a relaxed version of the formal cake from that cookbook but is still spectacular.*

INGREDIENTS

4 egg whites
pinch of sugar
1½ cups (345 g) caster sugar
1 teaspoon vanilla essence
1 tablespoon cornflour
90 g ground hazelnuts
⅔ cup (170 ml) cream
200 g dark chocolate, chopped
300 ml cream, whipped
2 punnets strawberries

Method

Preheat the oven to 180°C. Line 2 baking trays with baking paper.

Beat the egg whites with the pinch of sugar, then add half the caster sugar and beat for 5 minutes. Add the remaining caster sugar and beat again for 5 minutes. Add the vanilla and cornflour, and beat until combined. Gently fold in the ground hazelnuts

Spread a circle of the mixture onto each oven tray. Cook for 10 minutes, then reduce the oven to 150°C and cook for 1 hour. Cool.

Place the cream into a saucepan and bring to the boil. Remove from the heat and add the dark chocolate. Stir vigorously until smooth. Cool a little then spread on top of both meringues.

Spread the whipped cream onto both meringues. Arrange the strawberries over the cream and place one meringue on top of the other.

Kathy Barrington, Geilston Bay, TAS

THAI CORIANDER CHICKEN

Serves 4

Of Caucasian extraction, my parents lived and worked in Thailand during the '60s and '70s where I was born, and inherited my Thai nickname. My mother, a keen cook, was taught by a masterful woman named Khun Jumnien, who was our cook and so much more.

In return my mother taught her 'Western' fare (which is about as precise as 'Asian' fare)

Khun Jumnien and Mum always made our childhood birthday parties special with their craft; their love of food was instilled in me and my siblings, and now my boys (aged 9 and 6) are competent 'multi-cultural' consumers, preparers and demanders of same.

INGREDIENTS

Frying Paste

2 decent roots and stalks of
   fresh coriander
2 garlic cloves
4 peppercorns
large pinch of sea salt
large pinch of white sugar
chilli, to taste
small knob of ginger if in a
   Chinese–y mood;
3 tablespoons rice bran oil

400 g chicken or pork mince, or
   a combination
1 onion, thinly sliced
1 bunch thinly sliced leafy greens
   (or broccoli florets, zucchini
   slices or snow peas)

Sauce

2 tablespoons fish sauce
2 tablespoons oyster sauce
juice of ½ lime or lemon
pinch of sugar
1 cup (250 ml) chicken stock or
   water
dash of shao xing wine (if in a
   Chinese–y mood)
Steamed rice and extra fish sauce,
   to serve
coriander leaves, finely chopped

METHOD

To make the frying paste, pound the ingredients (except the oil) in a mortar and pestle or process in a small processor to a coarse consistency. Heat a wide frypan pan or wok to medium. Add the oil, then immediately add the frying paste, move it around with a spatula until fragrant. Try not to let it burn. Increase the heat to high and immediately add the mince and move around to cook thoroughly (if you prefer darker browned meat, sear it in the pan in small batches before lowering the heat to add the frying paste).

Add the vegies and stir-fry for a couple of minutes before adding all the sauce ingredients. Bring to the boil and simmer gently for a few minutes until the vegetables are just cooked. Adjust the sweet/salty/tart elements to taste. The sauce shouldn't be too much of one. Switch off the heat and toss through the coriander leaves.

Serve with steamed rice and extra fish sauce on the side.

Note: I use 1 fresh and deseeded bird's eye chilli so my boys can manage the heat, and I provide extra chopped fresh chilli soaked for 5 minutes in fish sauce on the side.

Alexandra 'Lek' Koswig, Mitcham, VIC

WEDDINGS

ABC Women's Session Christmas Cake

Serves 12–14

This recipe was written down by my mother from the ABC Radio Women's Program on December 1953. Since then it has been made for every family wedding, Christmas and christening. It is traditionally made with several family members helping. The butter and sugar are creamed by hand (in a large wash bowl) by an adult while the younger family members chop the fruit (with frequent sampling!). We converted the quantities to metric over the years.

Ingredients

500 g butter

500 g dark brown sugar

12 eggs

600 g flour — half plain and half self-raising, sifted

1 teaspoon bicarbonate of soda, sifted

1 dessertspoon ground cinnamon

500 g raisins

500 g sultanas

250 g glacé cherries

125 g chopped blanched almonds

125 g mixed peel

250 g figs, finely chopped

250 g dates, finely chopped

250 g prunes, finely chopped

250 g glacé apricots, finely chopped

juice and finely grated rind of a large fresh orange

½ cup (125 ml) brandy, rum or sherry

Method

Preheat the oven to 160°C. Grease a 28 cm cake tin and line with two thicknesses of heavy brown paper.

Cream the butter and sugar, and beat in the eggs, one at a time. When very light, add the sifted dry ingredients. Stir in the fruit. Lastly add the juice and spirits.

Bake for 3 hours on the bottom shelf in the oven.

Additional hints: Soak the raisins and sultanas in the brandy, rum or sherry overnight. Roll the cherries in flour. Other fruit, for example glacé pineapple or dried cranberries can be added. Add 1 tablespoon Parisienne essence to make the cake dark. Add 2 tablespoons of apricot jam to the mixture just before putting in the tin. As soon as it comes out of the oven sprinkle liberally with extra rum or brandy.

Judith Amey, Shenton Park, WA

CHAMPAGNE GINGERED FRUIT SALAD

Serves 8–10 (easily increased)

Fruit salad with champagne has long been a simple, easy and refreshing dessert for me to serve at parties in summer (great for a buffet), but it wasn't until I decided to add diced ginger that the accolades flowed. You can now buy glacé ginger which is already finely diced, making it much easier to add. It certainly does give it a distinct oomph. I like to macerate the fruit for some time, even overnight, to give it added appeal.

INGREDIENTS

2.5 kg fresh fruit
1 tablespoon finely diced glacé ginger
1 cup (250 ml) ice cold champagne or sparkling wine
1 tablespoon orange based liqueur (optional)
mint sprigs, to garnish

METHOD

Prepare the fruit as required and place into a large glass bowl. Add the ginger and stir to mix.

Combine the champagne and liqueur (if using), pour over the fruit and stir through.

Cover and refrigerate for at least 30 minutes or until ready to serve.

Decorate with sprigs of mint, and serve with ice cream, if desired.

Note: Choose from mangoes, peaches, nectarines, apricots, pears, rock melon, honeydew melon, papaya, kiwi fruit, passionfruit, strawberries, raspberries, blueberries, cherries, seedless grapes, lychees, apples (taking into consideration variety in colour). Remove stones where necessary, peel if required and cut into 2.5 cm cubes.

Judith Lynn Bell, by email

Coconut Cake
Serves 8–10

This is a special occasion cake because it is the best coconut cake that you will find — I don't know where I got the recipe from — I think I cut it out of a newspaper. I will use any occasion to make it because it is a rich, moist, lovely cake. I love it.

Ingredients

125 g butter
1 teaspoon coconut essence
1 cup (230 g) caster sugar
2 eggs
1 cup (90 g) desiccated coconut
1½ cups (225 g) self-raising flour, sifted
300 g sour cream
1 cup (250 ml) milk

Coconut Ice Frosting
2 cups (250 g) icing sugar, sifted
1⅓ cup (120 g) desiccated coconut
2 egg whites, lightly beaten
pink food colouring (optional)

Method

Preheat the oven to 180°C. Grease a deep 23 cm round cake tin line the base with paper; grease the paper.

Cream the butter, coconut essence and sugar with an electric mixer until light and fluffy. Beat in the eggs one at a time until combined. Add the coconut and flour with the sour cream and milk. Stir until smooth. Pour into the cake tin and bake for about an hour. Stand for 5 minutes before turning out onto a wire rack to cool. When cold, top with the frosting.

To make the frosting, combine the icing sugar and coconut with the egg whites and mix well. Add a little pink colouring if you wish.

Margaret Kavanagh, Moonee Ponds, VIC

Easy Mix Fruit Cake

Serves 8–10

I have used this recipe to create Christmas, wedding, birthday and any other type of celebration cake.

Ingredients

1 kg mixed fruit
50 g slivered almonds
good splash of sherry, port or brandy
2 tablespoons marmalade
2 cups (400 g) brown sugar
1 cup (250 ml) milk
250 g butter
3 eggs, lightly beaten
3 cups (450 g) plain flour
1 teaspoon each of ground ginger, nutmeg and cinnamon
1 teaspoon bicarbonate of soda

Method

Combine the fruit and nuts, pour over the sherry, port or brandy and leave to soak (at least overnight, or several days if possible).

Grease and line a 22–25 cm cake tin.

Add the marmalade and brown sugar to the fruit mixture.

Combine the milk and butter then heat until the butter has melted. Cool and add to the fruit mixture. Add the eggs, stir well and then stir in the sifted flour, spices and bicarb soda.

Place the mixture into the prepared tin in a cold oven. Turn the oven to 120°C and bake for 5 hours. This can vary with oven types.

The quantity of mixture is also enough for three 15 cm tins which are perfect for gift giving.

Jennifer Lehmann, Newtown, VIC

EREBOS AND NYX

Serves 2

After our wedding we found we had an excess of sparkling wine. At the same time the price of blackberries dropped dramatically giving birth to a special wedding cocktail that was named after the Greek deities of darkness and night, who gave birth to day and light.

INGREDIENTS
10 blackberries
50 ml creme de mure (blackberry liqueur)
40 ml Frangelico
35 ml cinnamon schnapps
sparkling wine, chilled
4 blackberries, for serving

METHOD
Muddle the blackberries in a shaker then mix with the liqueurs. Strain the liquid to remove the berry seeds.

Pour into 2 champagne flutes then top with bubbly. Float 2 blackberries in each glass and serve.

Anna Fedeles, Newtown, NSW

MAMA'S CHOCOLATE-STRAWBERRY DELIGHT

Serves 8–10

This is a cake-based dessert with a chocolate mousse topping over strawberries. A cake to be eaten on many a family occasion, including weddings, and invented by Mama about 70 years ago.

I have used this cake as a wedding cake by quadrupling the recipe and cooking it in the roasting pan. The filling can be varied according to what is in season.

INGREDIENTS

Cake
3 eggs, separated
2 tablespoons sugar
2 tablespoons cocoa powder
½ teaspoon ground cinnamon
200 g strawberries

Mousse
60 g dark chocolate
20 g butter
1 cup (250 ml) cream, whipped

METHOD

To make the cake, preheat the oven to 150°C and grease a 24 cm springform cake tin.

Beat the egg yolks and sugar until creamy, then sift in cocoa and cinnamon. Stir in gently. Fold in the stiffly beaten egg whites gently until combined. Place the mixture into the prepared tin and cook for 25 minutes.

Allow to cool. The cake will subside in the centre, where the strawberries are piled in.

To make the mousse, melt the chocolate and butter and stir until smooth. Pour into the whipped cream stirring until it forms the mousse. Arrange the mousse around the edge of the cake so the strawberries can be seen in the centre.

Jenny Shaw, by email

MUD CAKE
Serves 24–36

I adapted this recipe from one given to a friend of mine by a dietitian at a big public hospital. She must have prescribed it for people needing to go on a chocolate diet! I am frequently asked to make it for engagement parties or weddings. It cuts into small squares easily because it is so dense. I always use a good dark eating chocolate instead of cooking chocolate. The flavour is much better. For a 20 cm family cake, use one-third of the ingredients listed here and cook it at 170°C instead of 160°C.

INGREDIENTS

750 g butter
4½ cups (1.12 litres) hot water
750 g dark chocolate
6 eggs, lightly beaten
6 teaspoons vanilla essence
3 tablespoons brandy
4 cups (600 g) self-raising flour
6 tablespoons cocoa powder
2¼ cups (495 g) sugar

Ganache
400 g dark chocolate
1 cup (250 ml) cream

METHOD

Preheat the oven to 160°C. Grease and line a 28 x 33 cm (or 30 cm square) cake tin.

Melt the butter in a saucepan and remove from the heat. Add the hot water, broken up chocolate, eggs, vanilla essence and brandy and stir until the chocolate is melted and the mixture is smooth.

Sift the flour and cocoa into a large bowl and add the sugar. Stir to combine.

Bake for about 1¾ hours or until a toothpick inserted in the centre comes out clean. If the top starts to get too brown before the cake is cooked, cover loosely with a piece of foil.

Leave the cake in the tin until it is cold before turning out onto a wire rack. Remove the paper. Put the cake onto a cake board and ice with the ganache.

To make the ganache, break the chocolate up and put in a microwave-proof bowl together with the cream. Microwave on 50 per cent power for 2 minutes and stir to mix. If necessary, microwave on 50 per cent power another minute or until the chocolate melts. Keep checking every 30 seconds, stirring each time. As you stir, the chocolate will melt further. Allow to cool a little before pouring onto the cake and spreading over the top and sides with a non-serrated edged knife.

Set in the fridge.

Hazel Maria Hillier, by email

MUM'S CELEBRATION FRUIT CAKE
Serves 10–12

My mum has been making this cake for at least 60 years, and I guess her mother made it before her. I'm not sure when the first cake was made, but it has been enjoyed at many weddings, christenings, birthdays and Christmases over the years. It's delicious as an afternoon snack too, with a cup of freshly brewed coffee. It's a great favourite with family and friends, especially my dad.

INGREDIENTS

1 kg dried mixed fruit
1 cup (250 ml) rum
1 cup (250 ml) sherry
500 g butter
500 g brown sugar
2 tablespoons marmalade
5 jumbo eggs
1 dessertspoon golden syrup
1 teaspoon each vanilla essence, lemon essence and almond essence
1 tablespoon Parisienne essence
20 blanched almonds
10 glacé cherries
1 cup (150 g) self-raising flour
1 cup (150 g) plain flour
1 teaspoon each mixed spice, ground nutmeg and ground cinnamon
1 teaspoon instant coffee

Method

Soak the dried fruit in the rum and sherry for 1 week (at least). Stir gently once daily. Top up if desired. Leave covered.

Preheat the oven to 190°C. Grease a 23 cm cake tin and line with 3 layers of brown paper.

Cream the butter, sugar and marmalade with an electric mixer, until light and creamy.

Add the eggs one at a time. Beat well after each egg is added. Scrape the sides of the bowl with a spatula.

Add the butter and egg mixture, remaining wet ingredients, almonds and glacé cherries to the soaked mixed fruit (you'll need a large bowl). Stir gently. Sift the flours, spices and coffee powder over mixture. Stir gently, but thoroughly, making sure there are no air pockets.

Spoon the mixture into the prepared tin, and then tap the tin gently on the table to remove any further air pockets. Smooth the surface. Place on the middle shelf of the oven and cook for 1 hour. Reduce the temperature to 180°C. Continue cooking for a further 1 hour.

The cake should be cooked when a skewer comes out clean, and the cake has come away slightly from the edge of the tin.

Cool the cake in the tin before turning out. Pour 2 caps of rum over the cake before storing in an airtight container.

Jean Marlton, Proserpine, QLD

SPECIAL FRUIT CAKE
Serves 10–12

My mother made this cake for many years. I in turn have done so for 44 years. We have kept one in airtight tin for over 5 years and it came out just as well as when cooked. We kept one for 4 years for christening, from the wedding day. It was still in excellent condition. A really wonderful cake.

INGREDIENTS

1 kg mixed dried fruit
1 cup (250 ml) sherry
250 g butter
250 g brown sugar
4 eggs
½ cup (160 g) fig jam
2 cups (300 g) plain flour
¾ cup (115 g) self-raising flour
2 teaspoons cocoa powder
1 teaspoon mixed spice
¼ teaspoon salt

METHOD

Soak the fruit overnight in half the sherry.

Preheat the oven to 120°C. Line the base and sides of a 20 cm square cake tin with foil, coming 5 cm above the top of the tin.

Cream the butter and sugar, add the eggs and jam; beat well.

Sift the dry ingredients together. Sift about one-third into a very large bowl. Add the soaked fruit then sift in the remaining two-thirds and mix with a wooden spoon. When well mixed, spoon into the prepared cake tin. Cook for 3½–4 hours. Check for overbrowning, and cover with foil if necessary. When cooked, pour over the remaining sherry. Fold the foil down over the top, leave for at least 24 hours to cool. Remove from the tin, wrap in foil and leave for at least 3 weeks to mature.

B. Graham, Stoneville, WA

TOMATO PHILLY TARTLETS
Makes 36

This recipe was one that I first made up for my own engagement party some years ago, and it went down such a treat that I still keep getting requests. It always goes down well at parties of any sort. The challenge with these tasty treats is to stop at just one. These tarts are best made a day in advance as they are quite time consuming to make. They reheat very well, and can even be made weeks in advance and then frozen.

INGREDIENTS

3 punnets cherry tomatoes, finely sliced
1 red onion, finely diced
small handful basil, chopped
splash of olive oil
salt and freshly ground black pepper
3 x 250 g tubs softened cream cheese
4 sheets puff pastry

METHOD

Preheat the oven to 200°C. Line 2 oven trays with baking paper.

In a bowl mix together all the ingredients except for the cream cheese and the pastry.

Using an 8 cm biscuit cutter or drinking glass cut out 36 discs. Place onto the prepared trays.

Bake the pastry (to ensure even baking you should only cook one tray at a time, or swap shelves halfway through) for about 15–20 minutes, until slightly brown. Take the trays out, and with a spatula, flatten all the discs.

Put the cream cheese in a piping bag and put a small flattened dollop on each disc, ensuring most of it gets covered. Now spoon a little bit of the tomato mixture over the top of each disc and put the tray back in the oven for 20 minutes.

Bert Veldman, Byford, WA

VANILLA AND ROSEWATER CUPCAKES
Makes 24

My girlfriend and I made these cupcakes for my engagement party. They were so dainty that the boys were a bit hesitant to try them, but after one bite everyone was addicted. The soft rose flavours add a little elegance and they would work well as a substitute for a wedding cake if you wanted to go for individual serves instead.

INGREDIENTS

Cupcake
375 g butter, softened
1 teaspoon vanilla essence
2 teaspoons rose water
1 cup (230 g) caster sugar
5 eggs
1 cup (100 g) almond meal
1 cup (150 g) self-raising flour
1 cup (150 g) plain flour

Icing
1 cup (125 g) icing sugar
2 teaspoons rose water
1–2 drops pink food colouring
1 tablespoon milk

Method

Preheat the oven to 180°C. Grease two 12-hole patty tins. Line with paper cupcake holders.

To make the cupcakes, beat the butter, vanilla essence, rose water and sugar in a large bowl with electric beaters until very light and fluffy. Gradually beat in the eggs, one at a time. Be sure to beat well to allow good aeration. Stir in the almond meal and flours.

Drop heaped tablespoons of the mixture into the cupcake holders. Bake for about 30 minutes or until the cupcakes are lightly golden. Remove from the patty tin and cool on a wire rack.

To make the icing, sift the icing sugar into a bowl. Mix in the rose water and colouring. Once combined, gradually add the milk until you reach the correct consistency. Add more icing sugar if needed. Spread over the completely cooled cupcakes.

Anna Fedeles, Newtown, NSW

HOMECOMINGS

BAKED CHOCOLATE SOUFFLÉ
Serves 6–8

This is one of my favourite recipes. I don't know where my mother got it from, but it is so easy and scrumptious. When my house burnt down 5 years ago I lost the recipe and put a call out to the public for a copy of it. I received many chocolate soufflé recipes but not like Mum's. Fortunately my sister had a copy of it. I would now like to share it with everyone as it means a lot to me, and in these days of struggling families, at least this is cheap to make and really scrumptious with custard, ice cream or just by itself.

INGREDIENTS
600 ml milk
3 tablespoons sugar
1 cup (125 g) cocoa powder
1 teaspoon vanilla essence
1 cup (80 g) fresh breadcrumbs, from day old bread
2 eggs, separated

METHOD
Preheat the oven to 180°C.

Combine the milk and sugar in a saucepan and stir to dissolve the sugar. Bring to the boil. Mix in the cocoa, flavour with the vanilla and pour over the bread-crumbs. Cool.

Mix in the egg yolks. Beat the egg whites to firm peaks and fold into the mixture. Pour into an ovenproof dish, and stand the dish in a baking dish of hot water.

Bake for 30 minutes.

Barbara Free, by email

Bobotie (Curried Mince)

Serves 6

This is a favourite South African mince dish which has been handed down over the years in our family. My grandparents and mother were from South Africa and we used to have many of their delicious recipes used in our home. If you like you can use lemon leaves instead of bay leaves for the top of this dish.

Ingredients

2 onions, sliced into rings

olive oil, for frying

1 kg best beef mince

1 slice white or brown bread

1 cup (250 ml) milk

1 tablespoon curry powder

1 tablespoon sugar

2 teaspoons salt

½ teaspoon ground pepper

1 teaspoon turmeric

5 teaspoons vinegar

½ cup (60 g) seedless raisins

3 tablespoons fruit chutney

2 eggs

4 fresh bay leaves

Method

Preheat the oven to 180°C. Grease an ovenproof dish.

Sauté the onion in a little oil until golden. Add the mince and sauté until browned. Soak the bread in the milk. Squeeze out and reserve the milk. Crumble the bread into the mince mixture. Mix in the remaining ingredients except for the eggs, reserved milk and bay leaves. Place the mixture into the prepared dish.

Roll up the bay leaves and press upright into the meat mixture. Whisk the eggs and milk together and pour over the mince mixture. Bake for 45 minutes or until the topping is set and golden. Serve with rice.

Felicity Rooney, Sale, VIC

CHEEKY LICKEN PIE
Serves 4–6

This recipe was named by my sister. It started life as a broccoli and chicken tart, but when I swapped the broccoli for leeks a friend dubbed it Leaky Chicken Pie. When I asked my sister what she wanted me to make one year she answered Cheeky Licken Pie without thinking, and it has been Cheeky Licken ever since.

INGREDIENTS
2 sheets frozen puff pastry
1 tablespoon olive oil
1 large onion, diced
100 g lean bacon, chopped
500 g chicken thighs, cut into bite sized pieces
3 leeks, white part only, sliced
250 g sour cream
3 tablespoons lemon juice
sea salt and freshly ground black pepper
4 tablespoons breadcrumbs
milk, to glaze

METHOD

Preheat the oven to 180°C and lightly grease a 26 cm pie dish.

Thaw 1 sheet of the pastry and use to line the pie dish. Prick all over with a fork and refrigerate for 1 hour. Remove from the fridge, cover with baking paper and weights and bake blind for 12–15 minutes. Set aside to cool.

Thaw the second sheet of pastry.

Preheat the oven to 220°C. Heat the oil in a wide pan and lightly brown the onion, bacon and chicken. Add the leek, stir in the sour cream and lemon juice and season with a small amount of salt and plenty of black pepper. Let the mixture simmer for a minute or 2 or until the leeks are beginning to soften.

Sprinkle the breadcrumbs over the base of the cooled pastry and top with the cheeky licken mixture. Top the pie with the second sheet of pastry. Press lightly to seal the edges and trim to size. Prick with a fork and glaze with milk.

Bake for 20 minutes or until golden brown.

Marilyn Verheyen, Stafford Heights, QLD

CHORIZO ROAST CHICKEN WITH ALL THE GOOD STUFF

Serves 4

I'm a 19 year old student who lives away from home in a college. They kick us out for the Christmas holidays so when I come home, I love cooking for my parents. This year when I came home, I wanted to do something special, so I came up with a new way of doing roast chicken and they loved it. It's ridiculously simple, but the results are amazing. This is my homecoming chicken.

INGREDIENTS

1.6 kg chicken
2 tablespoons fresh thyme leaves
1 large chorizo sausage, thinly sliced
1 lemon, quartered
4 garlic cloves, peeled
6 medium potatoes, quartered
2 large carrots, cut into thirds
3 smallish onions, halved
6 garlic cloves, unpeeled
extra virgin olive oil
2⅔ cup (670 ml) white wine
2½ tablespoons plain flour

METHOD

Preheat the oven to 220°C.

Wash the chicken and pat dry with paper towels, then place on a chopping board and lift the skin from the breast. Using your fingers, push the thyme leaves and chorizo under the skin, spreading evenly. Cover the skin back over everything nicely.

Stuff the chicken cavity with the lemon quarters and peeled garlic, and place into an oiled baking dish. Arrange the vegetables and unpeeled garlic around the chicken. Brush the chicken all over with the oil and sprinkle with a little salt and pepper. Bake for 20 minutes then pour about 4 tablespoons white wine over the chicken. Put it back in the oven for another 20 minutes, then add 4 more tablespoons wine. Each time you add the wine, make sure you're pouring it over the legs of the chook as well as the breast. This will make the skin go really crispy. Bake for another 20 minutes or until golden brown.

Remove the chook to rest on a plate that will catch any juices. Put the vegies back in the oven until they are nicely browned, then arrange around the chicken and keep warm.

Leave the unpeeled garlic in the roasting tray and place onto the stove. Squash the garlic with a spoon until the sweet roasted insides come out, then discard the skins.

Don't worry about getting rid of the fat from the pan because it all tastes really good, just wait for the stove to heat up the pan to medium heat and then sprinkle the flour over. Stir for about 5 minutes, or until you have a golden brown paste. Add the remaining white wine and stir over high heat until the gravy boils and thickens. Add any juices that have accumulated on the plate that the chicken has been resting on.

Serve your beautiful chicken with the gravy, the roasted vegies and make sure you steam some greens as well — broccoli, beans or cabbage are my favourites. The lemon from the cavity of the chicken tastes pretty good too.

Kate Redman, Buderim, QLD

COQ AU VIN
Serves 4–8

Our family first tasted something like this in Souillac on the Dordogne in 2001. We have since spent some time trying and adapting various recipes, including Elizabeth David's, with ingredients available locally in Fremantle. This has now become a family favourite — the current version follows although I must admit it changes every time.

INGREDIENTS
1 onion, chopped
4 garlic cloves, crushed
2 lean bacon rashers, chopped
2 tablespoons extra virgin olive oil
2 carrots, chopped
6 large field mushrooms, chopped
1 bottle (750 ml) WA cabernet sauvignon
2 cups (500 ml) chicken stock
1 heaped tablespoon honey
chopped fresh herbs — basil, oregano, flat-leaf parsley
1 bay leaf
freshly ground black pepper
juice of 1 orange
8 large free-range skinless chicken thighs

Method

Gently fry the onion, garlic and chopped bacon in the olive oil then stir in the carrot and mushrooms. Cover and cook until the mushrooms begin to sweat then add the wine, stock, honey, herbs, bay leaf, pepper and orange juice.

Bring the mixture to the boil, then turn down the heat and simmer until the volume is reduced by half. Turn off the heat and allow to stand for at least an hour, or overnight in the fridge if convenient.

Preheat the oven to 160°C. Bring the mixture back to the boil and transfer to a casserole dish. Add the chicken and bake for 90 minutes.

Note: An interesting variation is to use dark chocolate instead of the honey.

Tom Hitchcock, Beaconsfield, WA

DAD'S FAVOURITE WITH THE KIDS AT HOME

My children are all old teenagers now, and one of them is a vegie head. A family feast is when they know that dad is making his favourite corned beef or lamb.

Place the beef or lamb into a large pot, cover with water and ½ cup of quality white wine vinegar. Add a few cloves and ¼ cup brown sugar. Simmer for 60 minutes a kilo and leave it to stand in the pot before carving — it melts in your mouth.

The vegies are all roasted (cooking separately from the meat feeds the vego as well). We like sweet potato, carrot, pumpkin, potato, capsicum and onion. A light sprinkle of herbs on the spuds adds colour and taste.

To make a light cheese sauce, melt a heaped tablespoon of butter and stir in a tablespoon of plain flour to make a paste. Gradually add 500 ml skim milk then 1 cup grated cheese. Simmer until thickened (boiling makes a mess and you have to start again!).

Dessert is a rhubarb and apple crumble cooked while the vegies are also in the oven. Homemade custard made by the person who did a good job on the sauce.

The best part about this meal is we all stand peeling the vegies and chatting, and keep chatting while the meal cooks.

Neil Worrell, WA

DONKEY DROPS
Makes 12–16

When my three daughters were young, I used to make these (minus coffee) for them on special occasions, such as their birthdays. The girls called these Donkey Droppings because of their appearance. As they grew up, they modified the name to Donkey Drops, and this has remained ever since. The girls are now in their thirties, yet they still ask for them on special occasions. I have been known to send Donkey Drops up to Canberra when my daughter was going through a difficult time and asked for my Donkey Drops to help her through.

INGREDIENTS

Biscuits
1 packet Granita biscuits, crushed
395 g can condensed milk
⅓ cup (30 g) desiccated coconut
⅔ cup (70 g) ground hazelnuts or almonds
½ teaspoon vanilla essence
3 level tablespoons cocoa powder
1 level tablespoon instant coffee

coconut or ground hazelnuts or almonds for coating

METHOD
Combine all the biscuit ingredients thoroughly. Roll into walnut-sized balls. Toss in the coconut or ground nuts. Enjoy!

Margaret Elizabeth Moloney, by email

FLORENTINE MEATBALLS
Serves 4

In the 'good old days', when we recycled our newspapers by taking them to the butcher, greengrocer or fish and chip shop, I rescued this recipe from around a bunch of garden-fresh carrots, and I've made it ever since.

INGREDIENTS

Sauce
1 large onion
2 carrots
1 celery stalk
3 tablespoons butter
1 tablespoon plain flour
2 cups hot beef stock
salt and pepper

Meatballs
500 g finely minced lean veal
250 g finely minced lean ham
1 teaspoon fresh thyme, chopped
2 tablespoons finely chopped
    parsley
1 garlic clove, crushed
2 eggs, lightly beaten
pinch of nutmeg
salt and pepper
plain flour

METHOD

To make the sauce, finely chop or grate the vegetables. Melt the butter in a large pot and sauté the vegetables until beginning to brown. Sprinkle with the flour, cook for a minute or 2 then stir in the hot stock and season to taste. Keep hot.

To make the meatballs, mix all the ingredients together (except the flour) and form into small balls, walnut to golf ball size. Roll in seasoned flour and drop into the simmering sauce. Cook for about 1 hour — stir gently from time to time to prevent sticking.

Serve with buttered spaghetti, a bowl of grated parmesan cheese and lemon wedges. Steamed broccoli or a green salad go well with this too.

Kit Clancy, Holbrook, NSW

FRANKFURTER TORTE
Serves 8–10

This is a third generation recipe, soon to become a fourth! It was originally made by my grandmother, Maria Kaiser, who was employed as a seamstress in the summer palace of Kaiser Wilhelm in Northern Germany, in the early 19th century. She would be asked specifically to make this cake for him. This recipe has been modified as her original states 12 eggs!

I have made it for all sorts of special occasions. With anticipation I would serve the first slice to my mother who, upon counting the layers and tasting, would pronounce it worthy of her merit! This cake has many links with our past, is full of emotional memories and is always made with much love and respect. And the best thing of all is that everyone who is fortunate enough to eat it absolutely loves it!

INGREDIENTS

Cake mixture
185 g butter
1⅔ cups (375 g) caster sugar
3 large or 4 small eggs
125 g plain flour
250 g self-raising flour
1 cup (250 ml) milk

Butter custard cream
4 cups (1 litre) thick sweet custard, cooled
butter, to taste

Coconut covering
2 cups (180 g) desiccated coconut
1 teaspoon sugar

METHOD

Preheat the oven to 180°C and grease a 25 cm ring tin.

To make the cake, beat the butter and sugar until creamy. Add the eggs one at a time, beating well. Fold in the sifted flours and milk alternately (it will be a fairly firm, shiny texture). Transfer to the prepared tin and bake for about 40 minutes, until golden brown and firm to touch. Turn out onto a wire rack to cool.

To make the butter custard cream, place one large 'dollop' of custard together with 1 tablespoon of butter in a bowl. Beat to a creamy, smooth consistency. Transfer to another bowl and continue beating custard and butter in small batches, tasting throughout to ensure a consistent taste is achieved. (The taste should lean towards the custard, not the butter.)

To make the coconut covering, combine the coconut and sugar in a nonstick pan. Stir over low heat until the coconut starts to brown. Do not be tempted to leave as the coconut can easily burn! Remove from the heat and keep stirring until the pan cools down. You are trying to achieve an even, well browned, crispy effect.

To finish off, a large work surface is essential! The cooled cake needs to be sliced at least 8 or 9 times. If the cake feels 'too fresh', place in the freezer for a short while to make it easier to slice. Don't worry if the slices are uneven as you can hide any imperfections with the butter custard cream! Lay the slices in sequence and, starting with the bottom, spread each layer with the butter custard cream. (It pays to have the first slice on the serving plate.) When all layers have been sandwiched together spread the butter custard cream all over the cake. Apply the coconut covering over the cake. This cake is best made the day before as the flavour becomes enhanced. It may look rich but is not so in taste!

Vilya Congreave

G'MA'S PIKELETS
Makes 26–30

My first granddaughter is now married, and working and living in Japan. When she comes to us at beautiful Wurtulla the first thing she wants is G'ma's Pikelets. Now her husband Kazuhisa loves them too. Pikelets have a very strong place in the Crane family history. Linda has eaten them all her life and our other 5 grandchildren love them too. Big kids eat them and wonder what the secret ingredients are!

INGREDIENTS

Date Spread
2 cups (320 g) chopped dried dates
1 teaspoon ground ginger
1 teaspoon ground cinnamon
½ cup (125 ml) orange juice

Pikelets
2 eggs
1 dessertspoon raw caster sugar (or white)
1 tablespoon plus 1 cup (150 g) self-raising flour
1 cup (250 ml) milk
½ teaspoon ground ginger
½ teaspoon ground cinnamon (grandma's magic ingredient)
1 tablespoon lemon juice

butter, for frying

Method

To make the date spread, boil all the ingredients until they form a soft spreadable consistency (or microwave for 3 minutes on high, stirring after each minute).

To make the pikelets, beat the eggs and sugar with rotary beaters. Add 1 tablespoon flour and the milk. Beat again for 1 minute.

Stir in the cup of flour, the spices and lemon juice using the beaters. This makes for a smooth batter. If too thick add a little more milk and stir again. You may use the batter immediately.

Heat a frying pan and lightly grease. Cook tablespoons of the batter, taking about a minute or so each side. I generally fit 8 in the pan each time and this makes about 26–30 pikelets.

Spread with butter or the date spread.

Dot Crane, Wurtulla, QLD

Ham Casserole Supreme
Serves 5 or 6

This recipe was adapted from The Hoosier Cookbook after we stayed in Indiana on a sabbatical leave in 1982–3. It was first used at a Homecoming Party for about 20 friends in Longueville in July 1983. It can easily be increased to cater for any number of hungry people!

Ingredients
½ cup (125 ml) milk
425 g can condensed cream of mushroom soup
2 teaspoons seeded mustard
3 spring onions, chopped
¼ teaspoon pepper
250 g fettuccine, cooked and drained
4 ham steaks, diced
1 cup (250 g) light sour cream
¼ cup (25 g) dry breadcrumbs or crushed potato crisps

Method
Preheat the oven to 180°C and grease a medium casserole dish.

Combine all the ingredients except the breadcrumbs or crisps. Pour into the prepared dish. Top with the breadcrumbs or crisps and bake for 20–25 minutes.

Geraldine Byrne, by email

JANE'S NANA'S AFGHANS
Makes 12–16

My nana used to make these yummy, chocolaty biscuits for me whenever I went to stay with her. No matter how old I grew, as soon as I arrived at her house I would head for the kitchen to find an old Tupperware container brimming with her Afghans. Now I make them regularly for friends and to take to work, and they are always a hit!

INGREDIENTS
220 g butter
⅓ cup (75 g) sugar
1 teaspoon vanilla essence
1 cup (150 g) plain flour, sifted
1 tablespoon cocoa powder, sifted
2 cups (60 g) cornflakes

Chocolate glaze
125 g dark chocolate
1 teaspoon butter
walnut halves, to decorate

METHOD
Preheat the oven to 175°C. Grease a baking tray.

Cream the butter, sugar and vanilla. Stir in the sifted flour and cocoa then the cornflakes.

Drop teaspoonfuls onto the prepared tray and bake for 15–20 minutes. Cool on a wire rack.

To make the chocolate glaze, melt the chocolate and stir in the butter. Spoon onto each biscuit and top with a walnut.

Jane Kenny, Cromer, NSW

LEMON CHICKEN WITH AVOCADO SAUCE

Serves 4

My peripatetic children all live in different states to me and one another, and they also spend a lot of time overseas (currently, one is in Canada, one in Papua New Guinea and the other has just come back from Japan), so there are often homecoming feasts in our family. The favourite homemade meal from Mum is the ubiquitous roast (a chicken stuffed with whole cloves of garlic and fresh herbs, and drizzled with soy sauce), but I recently tried one of my favourite easy-to-make meals on my eldest daughter. Her disappointment turned to sounds of delight and the greatest of all compliments, especially from a daughter, a request for the recipe!

INGREDIENTS

500 g chicken fillets (breasts or thighs)
paprika
sea salt and freshly ground pepper
dry breadcrumbs
2 tablespoons butter
1 onion, thinly sliced (or leeks/shallots)
2 garlic cloves
juice of 3 lemons
soy sauce

Avocado Sauce
1 avocado
squeeze of lemon juice
2 tablespoons mayonnaise
fresh herbs
sea salt and freshly ground pepper

METHOD

Preheat the oven to 180°C.

Slice the chicken into serving sized pieces. Put the chicken, with a dash of paprika and a sprinkling of salt and pepper, in a plastic bag, and shake together with enough breadcrumbs to coat the chicken. Place the chicken in a shallow baking dish.

Melt the butter in a small saucepan. Add the onion and garlic and cook until the onion is transparent. Add the lemon juice and a good dash of soy sauce to taste.

Pour the sauce over the chicken. Bake the chicken for 15 minutes, then turn the chicken pieces over and return to the oven for a further 15 minutes (thighs may take a bit longer).

While the chicken is cooking, make the avocado sauce. Mash the avocado in a small bowl. Add a squeeze of lemon juice and the mayonnaise. Stir in the fresh herbs and salt and pepper.

Serve the chicken on a bed of rice, spooning the lemon sauce over it and then topping with the avocado sauce. Serve it with freshly steamed vegetables of choice.

Stephanie Owen Reeder, by email

Mum's Best Chicken Recipe

Serves 1

This is a recipe my mum makes for me every time I go home to Adelaide. It never quite tastes the same when I make it at home. It is an adaption of something Mum found in a magazine and includes the way my Polish grandmother cooked egg noodles for us when we were small. She loves making it even though she doesn't eat chicken herself!

INGREDIENTS

2 chicken thigh fillets (we swear they are tastier than breast meat)
2 thin slices prosciutto
1 jar cranberry sauce
½ round firm camembert
little olive oil
good handful chopped spring onions
1 cup (250 ml) white wine
300 ml cream
egg noodles (ones from the Barossa Valley are great)
butter

METHOD

Preheat the oven to 180°C.

Remove excess fat and skin from the thigh fillets. Place the prosciutto on a chopping board. Open out the thigh fillets and place on top of each prosciutto slice. Smear a good amount of cranberry sauce on the fillet.

Cut the camembert into small wedges and place on top of the cranberry sauce. Roll up the chicken fillets carefully in the prosciutto and secure with toothpicks.

Heat the oil in a frying pan, add the chicken and cook until the prosciutto is crispy and chicken has browned. Remove from the pan and place into a baking dish. Finish cooking the chicken in the oven for about 10 minutes.

Place 3 dessertspoons of the cranberry sauce into the frying pan and heat with spring onions until they are soft.

Add the white wine and cook off. Add the cream and cook over low heat until reduced.

Cook the egg noodles as per directions on the packet, but slightly undercook.

Melt the butter in a frying pan and mix through the egg noodles until some of the noodles become crunchy.

To serve, place the egg noodles on a plate. Place the cooked chicken pieces on top of the noodles and pour the sauce over the top. Serve with a green salad.

Fiona Luestner, Penda, SA

MUM'S MUFFINS
Makes 12

I make these simple but scrumptious muffins for all homecomings — when family comes from a great distance or one of my daughters or a friend drops in for a serious chat (a comfort food chat — one that calls for something a bit more special than a biscuit!)

INGREDIENTS

1 cup (150 g) self-raising flour
1 cup (125 g) grated cheese
1 cup (250 ml) milk
1 tablespoon chopped fresh herbs (parsley, chives and garlic chives)
1 tablespoon pine nuts

METHOD

Preheat the oven to 200°C.

Mix the flour, cheese and milk. Add the herbs and pine nuts.

Spoon into greased muffin tins and cook for 15 minutes or until nicely golden. Remove from the tin and cool slightly. Split across the middle and butter. Make a pot of tea or coffee and provide a good listening ear!!!!

Varelle Hardy, by email

NANNY CAKES
Serves 8–10

My granddaughter Helen, who was 2 at the time, called these cakes 'nanny cakes' and the name has stuck. She and her family live in Wallacia, and Helen and her younger brother Ben sometimes spend school holidays with us. I always have to make 2 Nanny Cakes for them to take home. They like to take a slice in their school lunches each day.

INGREDIENTS
2 tablespoons sherry or port
500 g mixed dried fruit
1 packet glacé cherries
1 cup (220 g) sugar
1 teaspoon mixed spice
1 cup (250 ml) cold water
125 g butter or margarine
1 teaspoon bicarbonate of soda
2 eggs, lightly beaten
1 cup (150 g) self-raising flour
1 cup (150 g) plain flour

METHOD
Pour the sherry or port over the dried fruit and cherries, leave in a covered container in the fridge for at least 2 days

Preheat the oven to 180°C. Grease a 20 cm round or square cake tin and line with 2 layers of brown paper and 2 layers of baking paper.

Combine the soaked fruit, sugar, spice, water and butter or margarine in a saucepan. Bring to the boil and while hot, add the bicarbonate of soda. Allow to cool.

Stir in the eggs and flours. Pour into the prepared tin. Bake for 1¼ hours.

Thalia Phelps, Rowena, NSW

POMI RUSTICO
Serves 4

This recipe is a variation of the classic dish from the Abruzzi hills of Italy. For me it speaks of family and foundation, and, oh yeah, never stand between an Italian boy and his mama's cooking!

INGREDIENTS

⅓ cup (50 g) diced eggplant

4 medium tomatoes

⅓ cup (60 g) diced chicken breast

oil, for frying

½ cup (125 ml) water

1 cup (200 g) rice, cooked

⅓ cup (50 g) finely chopped onion

2 tablespoons grated carrot

grated cheese

olive oil

balsamic vinegar

chopped garlic

METHOD

Salt the eggplant lightly and put aside for about an hour.

Preheat the oven to 200°C.

Cut the tops off the tomatoes, scoop out most of the insides and save.

Season the chicken generously, and then fry in a lightly oiled pan over high heat. As the chicken browns, add the water. Drain this 'stock' into a bowl (repeat if necessary) for reuse and put the chicken aside.

Lightly oil the frying pan again, and the fry seasoned onion until soft and lightly brown. Add the grated carrot along with the eggplant cubes which have been drained and had excess moisture squeezed out.

Stir in the chicken, rice and stock, to make the mixture rissotto–like, adding more stock and water as required, with grated cheese of choice.

Spoon the rice mixture into the tomato 'bowls', and bake on a greased tray in the oven until the tomatoes are soft.

Serve on individual plates with a purée made from the reserved tomatos, the olive oil, balsamic vinegar and chopped garlic.

Suitable as an elegant entrée or light main course.

Luciano Battaglini, by email

POTTED BEEF
Serves 20

I was born in England towards the end of the war and I remember, as a young child, some of the rare treats we would occasionally find in the village grocer's shop. One of these was potted beef, to have at home on hot toast for supper. Many years later, as I recalled the aromas and tastes of those times, none of the so-called traditional recipes that I tried even came close. So with my mother's childhood memories to guide us, we came up with this version. Real potted beef, easy and tasty for picnics and lazy Sunday evenings.

INGREDIENTS
1 kg stewing beef, cut into bite sized cubes, trimmed of fat
125 g butter, cut into small cubes
45 g can anchovy fillets, drained and coarsely chopped
100 ml cold water
2 bay leaves
5 good pinches of freshly grated nutmeg
freshly ground black pepper

METHOD
Preheat the oven to 125°C.

Combine all the ingredients together in a heavy casserole dish, with plenty of freshly ground black pepper. Cover the dish and bake for 4 hours, stirring occasionally. Add a little more cold water if necessary, to keep the mixture moist.

Drain and reserve the liquid from the meat. Discard the bay leaves. Shred the meat with a pair of forks then chop it to a fine paste using a heavy kitchen knife.

Check the seasoning and add some more freshly ground black pepper if you wish. Mix the meat paste and reserved liquid together, and press this mixture firmly into storage containers. Cover the surface with a piece of baking paper, put a lid on the container, and refrigerate or freeze.

Notes: This needs to be well seasoned. So use lots of freshly ground black pepper. But you won't need to add salt as the anchovies provide the required saltiness.

Anchovies and nutmeg are essential to this dish. The taste of the anchovies blends in with the meat and won't be a problem for those who don't like them.

It is best to make potted beef a day or 2 in advance, to give the flavours time to develop. It will keep in the refrigerator for several days and for months in the freezer.

John Evered, Beaumaris, VIC

Prawn and Vodka Pasta
Serves 4

Recently our son returned home after a long absence working interstate. To celebrate the event we had a family dinner to catch up with what had been happening in each other's lives. For a main course I cooked this recipe, which was delicious, accompanied by a bottle of Tasmanian chardonnay. Each time I cook this meal I remember that special occasion.

Ingredients
3 tablespoons olive oil
1 small onion, finely chopped
250 g can tomatoes
1 garlic clove, crushed
3 tablespoons dry white wine
1 teaspoon tomato puree
a few sprigs rosemary and basil leaves
15 g butter
250 g peeled prawns
200 g button mushrooms
4 tablespoons vodka
75 ml double cream
spaghetti, cooked until al dente
vasil leaves, to garnish

METHOD

Heat 1 tablespoon of the oil in a frying pan. Add the onion and cook gently for about 5 minutes, stirring frequently, until softened. Add the tomatoes and garlic and stir the tomatoes well to break them up. Add the wine, tomato puree, rosemary and basil leaves.

Bring to the boil, then reduce the heat and simmer, uncovered, for about 15 minutes, stirring until the sauce is reduced to a thick puree. Remove from the pan and set aside.

Meanwhile heat the rest of the oil in the cleaned frying pan. Add the butter and heat until sizzling. Add the prawns and mushrooms, stirring well. Pour in the vodka, increase the heat and cook, stirring constantly, until all the liquid has evaporated.

Add the reserved tomato sauce and the cream and stir until well blended and heated through. Serve over the spaghetti and garnish with the basil leaves.

Robin Gardiner, Tranmere, TAS

ROAST BEEF AND BAKED RICE
Serves 4

This recipe has been passed down through generations of my late mother's family, through Spain, Holland, England and finally to Australia. It has evolved as it travelled — from beef baked on plain boiled rice to the delicious treat it is today — and is the only meal all of our family want, and expect, on their birthdays. It is a much-loved dish!

INGREDIENTS

1.5 kg piece beef bolar blade
garlic cloves, slivered
1 cup (155 g) frozen peas
1 onion, chopped

1½ cups (300 g) rice
2 teaspoons dried mixed herbs
salt and sugar
olive oil

METHOD

Preheat the oven to 180°C.

Make deep cuts in the beef and insert the slivers of garlic into the cuts. Set aside.

Combine the peas and onion in a saucepan, cover with water and cook until tender; take off the stove.

Place the rice and herbs into a medium sized flameproof baking dish and season with a little salt and sugar. Cover with water and stir over medium heat until the water is absorbed.

Drain the liquid from the cooked peas and onion onto the rice, and again keep stirring until absorbed. Mix the peas and onion in with the rice. Adjust seasonings.

Place the beef on top of the rice, rub with oil, and bake for about 1½ hours, or until done to your liking. During cooking time, the rice crisps around the sides of the dish, and the beautiful juices from the beef drip onto the rice. Every 30 minutes, take from the oven and use a spatula to move the crisp rice into the middle and the middle bits to the side, and turn the beef. Serve with gravy, and baked and/or green vegies.

Claudia Miriam Monson, Port Sorell, TAS

Soldier eggs
Serves 1

This recipe is from my pop. He used to make it for me every weekend when I used to stay at his house as a kid. He would bring it on a tray while I watched cartoons. It is simple but comforting and reminds me of his patience and kindness. He taught it to me years later and it is a meal I will never forget as it brings fond memories.

Ingredients
2 eggs
salt and pepper
2 slices white bread, toasted
butter
dash of cream
butter

Method
Poach the eggs until they are just soft in the middle; drain. Add a good dash of pepper and salt, and a small amount of butter and cream. Mash roughly with a fork.

Spread onto 2 pieces of buttered white toast (important), and cut into 4 soldiers (important).

Kelly Lyons, by email

SHIRLEY KINROSS'S GINGERNUTS
Makes 16

Shirley Kinross lived in the beautiful Victorian country town of Maldon. She worked in the hospital as a young woman and raised a family there. She was active in the community, helping to raise funds for the school, fire brigade, hospital, elderly citizens — you name it, she was there to help. Her garden always had wonderful flowers for picking; to take to friends or decorate the hall for a dance or celebration. She was a good cook who took pride in her baking, and was generous with advice and recipes. This one was written out on a library card for me a few months before she died. I make them often and remember her spirit and her great love of life.

INGREDIENTS

125 g butter
1 cup (220 g) sugar
1 tablespoon golden syrup
1 egg (60 g), lightly beaten

2 cups (300 g) self-raising flour
½ teaspoon bicarbonate of soda
4 teaspoons ground ginger

METHOD

Preheat the oven to 180°C and grease a baking tray.

Melt the butter, sugar and golden syrup in a saucepan over low heat. Cool slightly and add the egg.

Sift all the dry ingredients and combine with the butter mixture. Form into a block and cool in the fridge for about 15 minutes, until firm. Roll teaspoonfuls into balls and place onto the prepared tray. Bake for 10–15 minutes. Remove from the tray and cool on a wire rack.

Note: The mixture may be rolled out and cut into various shapes. I like to make hearts and pack them in cellophane for gifts. They can be iced and used to make edible decorations for the Christmas tree.

Jeanette Fry, Richmond, VIC

SIMPLY MAGIC MOUSSE
Serves 6

My mousse has become a favourite homecoming dessert for my friend's children. When they visit from Brisbane and America, the one request I get when I visit their family farm is to bring the mousse. Now three generations are enjoying the mousse and it is also a favourite dessert among many of my friends.

INGREDIENTS
200 g Toblerone chocolate
2 large eggs
2 cups (500 ml) cream

METHOD
Break up chocolate and reserve 2 sections. Place the chocolate into a heatproof bowl and melt over hot water or in the microwave. Do not let the chocolate come into contact with the water. Stir until melted.

Place the eggs into a saucepan and whisk over low heat until tepid and frothy, add the melted chocolate and beat until smooth.

Whip the cream until it holds soft peaks and then fold through the chocolate mixture.

Place into small bowls or a medium bowl. Chop the remaining chocolate and sprinkle over the mousse, then place into the freezer. Remove from the freezer 30 minutes before serving.

Leonie Clarke, by email

Tuna Rice Soufflé

Serves 4

One day during the 1960s, we are not exactly sure of the year, my mother went to a cooking demonstration at the old Gas and Fuel building in the city. She brought home this tuna rice soufflé recipe and it has remained a firm favourite with our family over the past 40 years. Even after my sister and I were diagnosed as coeliacs several years ago, we have continued to make it, as the flour in the filling can be easily substituted with gluten-free flour.

Ingredients

Rice base
1 cup (200 g) long-grain rice, cooked
30 g butter
1 egg
Salt and pepper
2 tablespoons chopped parsley
425 g can tuna, drained

Filling
120 g butter or margarine
1 large onion, finely chopped
½ cup (75 g) plain flour
2 cups (500 ml) milk
¾ cup (90 g) grated cheese
2 eggs
½ cup (125 ml) cream
1 teaspoon dry mustard
2 teaspoons lemon juice
grated cheese, extra
dry breadcrumbs, to sprinkle

Method

Preheat the oven to 180°C.

To make the rice base, mix the rice, butter, egg, salt and pepper and parsley together and place in an oblong ceramic or glass baking dish. Arrange the tuna over the rice mixture.

To make the filling, melt the butter or margarine in a saucepan, and add the onion. Sauté until transparent. Add the flour and stir until smooth and bubbling; blend in the milk.

Stir constantly until the mixture boils and thickens. Remove from the heat and cool slightly. Add the grated cheese, eggs, cream, mustard, and lemon juice. Stir until the cheese melts.

Pour the mixture over the rice and tuna.

Sprinkle some extra grated cheese over the top with some breadcrumbs (gluten free if needed).

Bake for 90 minutes or until golden brown.

Elizabeth Brookes, Blackburn, VIC

VERENIKI
Makes 20–30

This recipe is a family tradition, passed down from generation to generation, and always served at family get-togethers. I can remember as a little girl going to Nana's house for a family lunch on Sunday after church. The kitchen windows would be all steamed up and you could smell the onions a mile away. Walking in, you would see hundreds of vereniki lined up on the tabletop ready to be cooked. We would all pitch in with the cooking — and especially the eating!

INGREDIENTS
2 cups (300 g) plain flour
1 egg, lightly beaten
½ cup (125 ml) water
salt
6–7 medium potatoes, boiled and drained
1 large onion, chopped and sautéed in oil
60 g butter, melted

METHOD
Mix the flour, egg, water and salt in a bowl to make a dough. Knead and set aside.

Mash the potatoes and add some of the onion.

Take a small ball of the dough and roll out to form a circle to fit in your palm. Put a small spoonful of the potato mixture into the centre of the circle, and press the sides together around the potato. Repeat with the remaining dough and filling.

Drop the vereniki into boiling water and cook for 7–10 minutes. Drain and serve with the remaining onion, and the melted butter.

Elizabeth Davey, by email

Index